# The Borris Lace Collection

## A UNIQUE IRISH NEEDLELACE

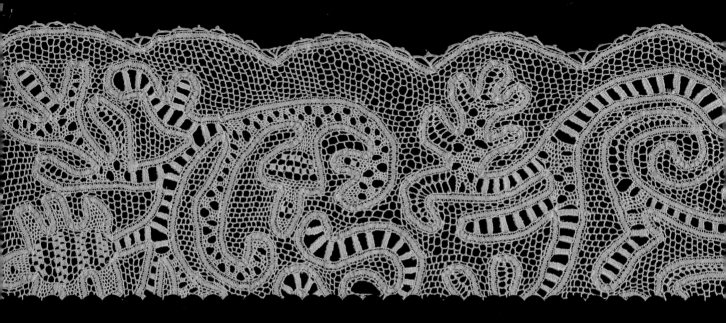

to the Kavanagh family,

*past, present and future.*

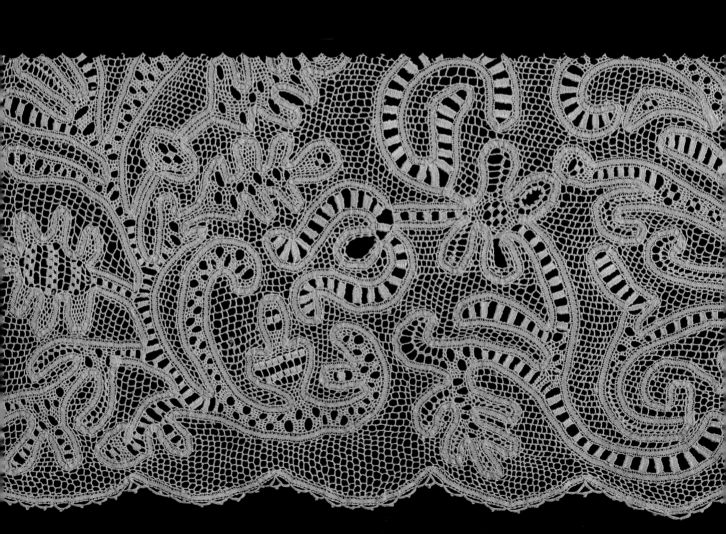

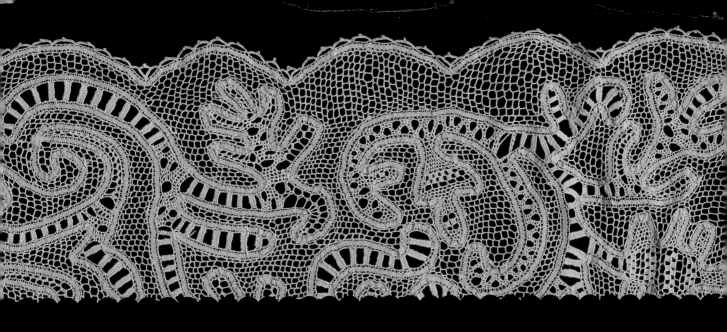

# The Borris Lace Collection

## A UNIQUE IRISH NEEDLELACE

### Marie Laurie & Annette Meldrum

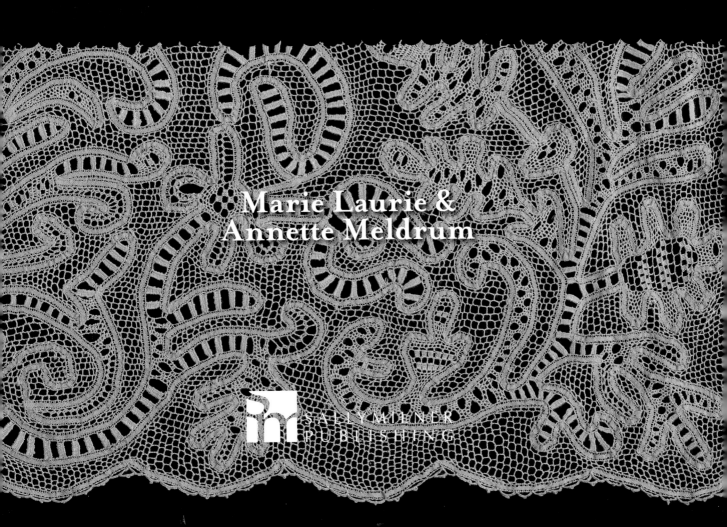

SALLY MILNER PUBLISHING

First published in 2010 by
Sally Milner Publishing Pty Ltd
734 Woodville  Road
Binda NSW 2583 AUSTRALIA

© Marie Laurie and Annette Meldrum 2010

Design: Caroline Verity
Editing: Anne Savage
Photography: George Meldrum
& projects photographed by Tim Connolly
Illustrations: Wendy Gorton
& Anna Warren, Warren Ventures Pty Ltd

Printed in China

National Library of Australia Cataloguing-in-Publication data:
    Author: Meldrum, Annette.
    Title: The Borris lace collection: a unique Irish needlelace / Annette Meldrum, Marie Laurie.
    ISBN: 9781863514071 (pbk.)
    Notes: Includes index.
        Bibliography.
    Subjects: Lace and lace making--Ireland--Borris.; Needlepoint lace--Ireland--Borris.
    Other Authors/Contributors: Laurie, Marie, 1935-
    Dewey Number: 746.2240941882

**Disclaimer**

Information and instructions given in this book are presented in good faith, but no warranty is given nor results guaranteed, nor is freedom from any patent to be inferred. As we have no control over physical conditions surrounding application of information herein contained in this book, the author and publisher disclaim any liability for untoward results

# ❋ acknowledgements

We would like to publicly thank Mr and Mrs Kavanagh for their support and assistance. We feel very privileged to have been allowed this opportunity to catalogue and study the Borris Lace Collection.

To Bobby Smith of Lorum, County Carlow, for her initial and subsequent introductions to the Kavanagh family and the lace collection at Borris House and for showing us her own treasured pieces of Borris lace.

We are also grateful to the Australian Lace Guild who showed their early confidence in our project by granting us the Jennie Fisher Scholarship in 2006–2007, which assisted with travelling expenses. In return, we presented a talk on Borris lace at the Lace Guild AGM in Perth in 2007 and a workshop at the AGM in Brisbane in 2008. We are also grateful to our first workshop participants for their encouragement and feedback.

To George Meldrum for his patience, understanding and constant support, and for his excellent photography.

To Rosemary Shepherd, retired lace curator, Powerhouse Museum, Sydney, for sharing her expert knowledge and identification of the bobbin lace items in the Borris Lace Collection.

To Barbara Ballantyne for her suggestions, references and thorough research of Irish lace history.

To Christine Bishop for her generous support and research assistance.

To Garry Searle for technical support.

To Jean Leader (UK) for bringing Ballantrae lace to our attention and sharing her knowledge.

To Father John, Sacred Heart Catholic Church in Borris, for showing us the Borris lace altar cloth and allowing us to photograph it on the church altar.

The late Nellie O'Cleirigh, Irish lace historian and author, who provided hospitality and access to her personal library and research while we were in Dublin. Her early research and articles laid the groundwork of our research.

Alex Ward, Assistant Keeper, National Museum of Ireland, Collins Barracks, Dublin for showing us the Borris lace in the museum collection.

Olwyn Scott, curator at The Lace Place, Hyden, Western Australia, for sending details of tape lace from the collection.

Allison Hill and Kerry Taylor for their careful proofing of our text and instructions.

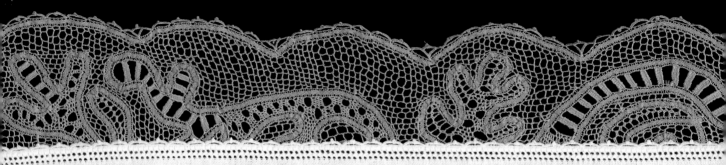

# ✳ contents

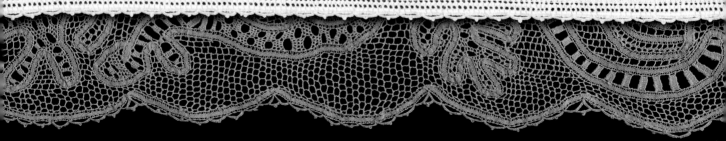

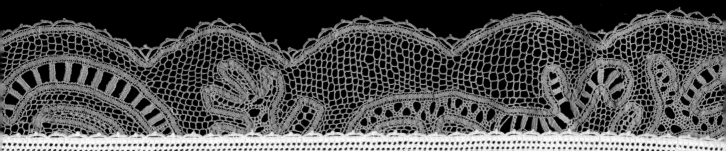

## PART III: PROJECTS

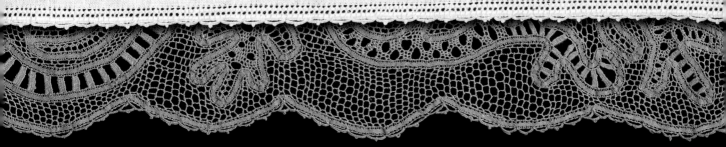

## ❋ foreword

Marie Laurie and Annette Meldrum have made a huge contribution to Irish lacemaking in producing this book.

*Borris House*

When Lady Harriet Kavanagh brought back samples of lace from her travels in the Adriatic, and decided to set up a cottage industry in Borris, the idea that two women from Australia would be cataloguing and researching this industry in one hundred and fifty years' time would have been unthinkable. Borris lace has certainly travelled since the days when the women of Borris sat outside their cottages, making full use of the daylight, as they toiled to supplement the family income. Marie, whose own mother's family had been craft workers in Ireland, has breathed new life into this nearly forgotten skill.

I hope this book will encourage others both in Australia and Ireland, to continue with this wonderful tradition of lacemaking. It is a living monument to the women who worked for the survival of their families during the Irish Famine.

*Mrs Tina Kavanagh*
CURRENT FAMILY CARETAKER OF THE
BORRIS LACE COLLECTION:
REMNANTS OF THE BORRIS LACE INDUSTRY

# introduction

------------------------------------ ❈ ------------------------------------

## HOW TWO AUSTRALIAN LACEMAKERS
## BECAME INVOLVED

〜 **Marie first became** aware of Borris lace from a chance conversation with a visiting relative from Ireland in the early 1980s. Borris lace is a little-known tape lace produced in the small town of Borris, County Carlow, Ireland between 1846 and the 1960s. When the industry closed, all unsold stock, materials and records were packed away in Borris House and forgotten except for the mounting of an occasional small exhibit at local events. After Marie's first visit to see the lace at Borris House in 1985, she contacted Susan Cox, principal of The English Lace School, 1979–1989 (located first in Tiverton, and later Rockbeare, both in Devon), and encouraged her to investigate the lace for inclusion in the Lace School curriculum. Subsequently a Mrs Corrigan from Borris travelled to Rockbeare to teach a once-only class in Borris lace. On Marie's second visit to Borris she met Mrs Corrigan and was given a brief lesson in using one of Mrs Corrigan's own patterns drawn onto blue roller-blind fabric. Marie has completed the piece and still has the original pattern.

In 2006 Marie and I visited Ireland together and arranged an appointment

with Mrs Tina Kavanagh, the caretaker of the Borris Lace Collection, to see the lace. Mrs Kavanagh was keen to know more about the lace in her care and to have it documented so that a more meaningful display could be mounted when opportunities presented, and encouraged us to return to Ireland to catalogue and document the collection, record the story and organise safe conservation storage to ensure its long-term preservation.

We returned in September 2007 to spend a week at Borris House, photographing, conserving and cataloguing. We shared our knowledge with each of the family members we met during our visit so that they have a clearer understanding of the significance of the collection as a very comprehensive Irish lace collection, as well as being of importance to the village of Borris and the Kavanagh family. We hope that our efforts have contributed to the long-term survival of the collection and give it a much higher status in the minds of future generations. The collection is available for viewing by appointment in the small family chapel attached to Borris House. An article we

# ※ introduction

wrote about our work was published by the Guild of Irish Lacemakers in their *Irish Lace Journal*, Spring 2008.

Borris House also has a nationally significant collection of estate records.[1] In addition to its historical value, the Borris Lace Collection is important as a remarkable example of Ireland's cultural excellence and lacemaking heritage. It is also important as one of many philanthropic enterprises set up to relieve hardship in Ireland in the mid 1800s.

In recent years, Australians have made a huge contribution to the documented research of little-known textile techniques. Effie Mitrofanis' *Casalguidi Style Linen Embroidery* and Marie Laurie's manual on *Hungarian Needlepoint Halas Lace: An Australian Interpretation* are prime examples. With little in the way of history and unique textile traditions in our own country, it seems that we eagerly seek out the textile traditions of other cultures.

Marie's love of tape lace inspired her to persistently involve herself in promoting and researching Borris lace. It is fitting that together we are recording the technique so that it will never again be lost and forgotten. We hope that the publication of this book will help to reclaim this beautiful lace from its undeserved obscurity and restore it to its proper place in the history and context of Irish laces.

Mr and Mrs Kavanagh of Borris House have given their unreserved approval to the publication of this book on the Borris Lace Collection. It is unfortunately not as exhaustive as we would like to have produced, Australia's distance from Ireland and the collection having limited the scope of our research. We have endeavoured, however, to bring together the little that is known and has been previously published with new research and the thorough documentation of the remaining collection.

*Annette Meldrum*
*Marie Laurie*

# PART I

the untold **story**

## BORRIS, COUNTY CARLOW, REPUBLIC OF IRELAND

Borris is a small Georgian town nestled in the fertile valley of the river Barrow, below the curve of the Blackstairs Mountains in County Carlow in south-east Ireland. The town's high street runs alongside the stone wall which borders the estate of the McMurrough Kavanagh family.

The imposing gatehouse of Borris House, one of Ireland's most important country houses, faces a small group of village shops in the middle of the high street.

The McMurrough Kavanagh family can trace an amazing lineage going back to the Celtic kings of Leinster, a large province in the east of Ireland which included the county of Carlow.

The present Borris House, the home of the Kavanagh family, was built in 1731 and is set in 600 acres of parkland and ancient oak woodland. It comprises three floors with wonderful stonework and is Tudor Gothic in style. It is in fact, more like a castle than a house.

Visit the website and see for yourself: http://www.borrishouse.com/history.htm.

*From top: map of Ireland showing the location of the small granite-built village of Borris; gatehouse to the Borris estate; Borris High Street.*

# Poverty is the mother of the Irish lace industry. History of lace-making in Ireland is more or less the history of Irish distress. *(Robinson 1887; unknown 1883)*[1]

## MODERN IRISH NEEDLELACES

**Borris point lace** is a tape lace, one of the many 'modern' Irish needlelaces developed in the nineteenth century to relieve the hardship which followed the Great Famine by making the poor women of Ireland and their households more economically self-reliant and independent of charity. In many cases, the laces evolved as a result of the clever study and copying of old laces from Europe by philanthropic Irish women. Lace was highly fashionable in Victorian times and the advent of the crinoline, which required large quantities of lace to trim each garment, gave a further boost to the industry.[2]

> The early specimens of lace were beautiful pieces of workmanship, comparable to the mediaeval 'guipures' and 'old points' of continental celebrity; they were in fact, imitations of them. The attempts to resuscitate their styles, and to rival their reputation, were by no means contemptible. Great aptitude for this revival was displayed. The art was easily acquired, the materials were inexpensive, and the market was ready.[3]

Numerous local schemes were set up by patrons, who might be the lady of the estate, other ladies of means, the wife of a clergyman or the Reverend Mother of a convent. Sometimes schools were organised to teach the local girls but more often the teaching was the work of nuns in the convent schools. Nineteenth century lace historian Mrs Bury Palliser wrote that after the Great Famine of 1846, the year of the commencement of the Borris Lace Industry, 'various lace schools were set up in different parts of Ireland, where lace was made with great success'.[4]

The success of these schemes was most often due to the clever ways in which their patrons connected the creative output of the women in the cottage industries or schools under their supervision with the tremendous wealth and buying capacity of the aristocracy with which they were connected. Lace was a highly marketable item to the wealthy as it signified wealth and privilege – 'even royalty did not disdain to adorn itself with Irish Lace'.[5]

Two Irish laces from this period, Limerick and Carrickmacross, which are embroidered onto machine-made net, have become extremely well known internationally. Borris lace, which is unlike any of the other Irish needlelaces, utilises machine-made lace tape which is sewn to a pattern, the elements of the naïve designs being held together by picoted bars or a net ground. Decorative filling stitches are used as a highlight and to fill the open areas of the design. Borris point lace was a forerunner of the 'modern' tape laces, which are dated by most lace historians from the 1860s on.[6]

# EARLY TAPE LACES

↝ **The practice of** sewing a straight woven tape onto a pattern was first employed by lacemakers in Milan and Genoa in the seventeenth century in what was described as mezzo punto, or half point, where half the work utilised a pre-made cloth tape, either woven or bobbin made, with the remainder consisting of needlelace fillings.[1] It was an attempt to make the production of lace faster and more economical. These tape laces were produced throughout the seventeenth and eighteenth centuries.

'The manufacture of braids was an important craft in medieval Europe'; they were produced domestically, in workshops, and also made by noblewomen as a leisure activity.[3] In Italy the production of constant-width tape dates from at least the seventeenth century. We know that prior to 1885, fine quality, loom-woven linen tape was produced in Holland and that twilled Indian tape was available, although it was rather stiff.[4]

*Section of a cuff of early Borris lace Image Coutesy of the National Museum of Ireland*

Pat Earnshaw notes that the tape for Borris Lace 'was at first made by hand, either in Genoa stitch giving a plaited braid effect, or in clothstitch by bobbins'.[5] Judyth Gwynne, in *The Illustrated Dictionary of Lace*, writes that in Borris lace only handmade tape from Genoa was used[6], but as very few early examples survive we can't be certain what this Genoese tape was like. It may have been similar to a narrow, heavy, flat woven twill tape seen in an early cuff of Borris lace held in the Dublin Museum, which resembles the twill weave produced by tablet weaving. Dated 1868, the cuff, in a vermiculated design, was purchased by the museum in 1914; it is made of silk and measures 4 x 17.5 cm. This tape certainly displays the plaited braid effect described by Pat Earnshaw.

Though the early tapes were hand-woven, it was not long before machine-made tapes were available. Woven tape of even width was one of the earliest products of the machine age.[7] As early as the late 1860s machine-made tape was available for ordering from Paris,[8] and by the last quarter of the century there was heavy demand for commercial tape. As tape laces gained popularity, towards the end of the nineteenth century some fifty varieties of machine-made tapes were being produced and widely used.[9] All the tape in the Borris collection appears to be machine made. Many of the fancy tapes found in the collection are no longer manufactured, but can be seen in old point lace pattern books. Today it can be difficult to obtain even the plain fine tape required for Borris lace. No bias tapes were ever used.

## TAPE LACE RESURGENCE

꙰ **Tape lace began** to resurface around 1840, having not been made since the late 1700s, and came to be known as point lace or point lacet ('lacet' simply means a narrow tape).[1] The availability of machine-made tape made the lace much faster and less difficult to produce. Fashion lace could be made by amateur needlewomen of all classes and ability for pleasure or income, and became popular throughout Europe and America. Borris lace seems to have been one of the earliest tape laces of the revival. Its production in Ireland precedes the introduction of tape lace into England by six years. It also predates the appearance of the major needlework publications which later provided unlimited patterns and instructions for tape laces.[2] In 1848 the first of Mlle Riego de la Branchardiere's many point lacet pattern books was published in London.[3] Many of her designs reflect a strong resemblance to pieces in the Borris Collection. Many point lace designs also appeared in The Queen, which was published from 1861.[4] The Needlecraft series of the Manchester School of Embroidery, and other point lace manuals produced around this time, include designs which show similarities to lace pieces in the Borris Lace Collection.

It seems doubtful, however, that these publications were an early influence on Borris lace. Mlle Riego

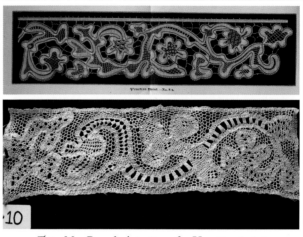

Top: Mrs Douglas's pattern for Venetian point
Above: Borris lace, Catalogue item no. 10

confidently claimed to be the 'inventress' of lace-like crochet and point lace,[5] but this claim in relation to Irish crochet has been questioned by Barbara Ballantyne's thorough research.[6] Similarly, I have not seen any evidence of this claim in relation to Borris point lace. Although Nellie O'Cleirigh wrote that the working instructions 'presumably … were similar to those used by Riego de la Branchardiere'[7], this is not the case, and certainly the stitch suggestions were not copied as in most cases they were not the usual stitches of Borris lace. The designs and edgings are the only similarities. Mlle Riego's designs and other designs of the time may, however, have contributed to later developments in Borris lace. For example, Pattern no. 8 in Mrs Douglas's Point Lace Book bears a very strong resemblance to Catalogue item no. 10.[8]

| COMMENCEMENT DATES FOR VARIOUS IRISH LACES | |
| --- | --- |
| Carrickmacross lace | 1820 + |
| Limerick tambour (later Limerick needlerun) | 1829 + |
| Irish crochet | 1845 + |
| Borris lace (thriving industry for over 100 years) | 1846–1960s |
| Youghal lace | 1852 + |
| Kenmare lace | 1861 + |
| Inishmacsaint lace | 1865 + |
| Kinsale lace | 1888 + |
| Bandon lace | 1920–1931 |

## THE ORIGINS OF BORRIS LACE

✢✢ **Nowhere in Ireland** was there more hardship experienced at the time of the Great Famine (1846–1848) than in the southern districts around Borris. The effects of the distress caused by the failure of the potato crops lasted for many years. Lady Harriet Kavanagh (1799–1885), the mistress of the Borris estate, realised that she had the connections to enable her to market a lace product, and a number of women on the estate who were in dire need of support and 'noted to be good workers of plain work'.[1]

Family legend has it that Lady Harriet so impressed with the designs in the old Greek lace that she saw when visiting Corfu, which was 'endeared to her by many ties', that she brought back some examples with the idea that they could be copied.[2] (Despite the romance of this story there are no pieces of Greek lace among the 'old family laces' in the collection). Corfu lace itself is described as a 'coarse Greek lace of little value or artistic beauty' so it is unlikely that it was this lace that caught Harriet's eye.[3] Similarly, legend surrounding the history of Ruskin lace has it that John Ruskin brought back from Italy specimens of 'so-called Greek lace'.[4] Confusingly, Greek point lace was sometimes given the name Venetian guipure;[5] 'old conventual' lace from Italy was also referred to as 'Greek lace',[6] and tape lace was known by a number of names including 'imitation Greek lace'.[7] Lace historian Pat Earnshaw nicely sums up the situation when she refers to the 'mystifying use of "Greek" lace which may never have been connected with Greece at all'.[8] We believe there is no reason to perpetuate the 'Greek myth' that seems so embedded in the few references available to Borris lace.

It was said by early twentieth century lace historian Mrs R.E. Head that 'Mid-Victorian travellers in Italy were able to obtain almost any quantity of these peasant laces for a moderate consideration' and later by Emily (Mrs F.N.) Jackson that 'English ladies buy a scrap of lace as a souvenir of every town they pass through'.[9] The old laces which we found in the collection at Borris House and which we refer to as the Kavanagh 'family lace' are possibly the pieces brought back by Harriet from her frequent trips to her beloved Neapolitan Riviera.[10] Down through history laces have been named after the town where they were made or the place where they were purchased.[11] In this case the pieces could have been purchased in Corfu or Italy or anywhere else. Lady Harriet travelled widely, even touring the Nile sites in the mid 1840s and bringing back a substantial number of antiquities which now form part of the Egyptian collection of the National Museum of Ireland.

It is well documented that all the various laces made in Ireland are copies of foreign laces and that no lace is actually indigenous to Ireland.[12] Borris lace is no exception, and Lady Harriet may have been well aware of this when she embarked upon her lacemaking

*It is well documented that all the various laces made in Ireland are copies of foreign laces and that no lace is actually indigenous to Ireland.*

enterprise. Evidence that designs continued to be copied from old lace is provided by a handwritten note on one of the patterns found in the collection: 'Taken from an old piece of "Greek"? pillow lace of Miss Buchanan's, Cornwall August 1923'.

As well as the patterns, the names of the old laces were also copied, which adds to the confusion.[13] Indeed, various articles in The Times of London record this: the report of an exhibition of Irish lace at Devonshire House in 1909 made special mention of Borris lace, 'which is in fact a modern reproduction of "Point de Milan" ... copied from beautiful old Italian models'; in 1905, a 'collar of lacet lace from the Borris Lace Industry, made in imitation of Genoese lace with a fine tape foundation'; and in 1911 Borris lace was mentioned as reproducing the beautiful designs and stitches of old Milanese lace.[14] Many imitations of seventeenth century Milanese lace were made in the later part of the nineteenth century.[15] The suffragist Helen Blackburn, in her Handy Book of References for Irishwomen, included a sales list of Borris lace items named to reflect such origins:

> Flounce of Point de Venice,
> *11 inches wide, 26s a yard;*
> Flounce of Point de Milan,
> *11 inches wide, 12s 6d a yard;*
> Child's collar and cuffs,
> *10s 6d; narrow laces, 9s to 21s a yard.*[16]

It appears that imitating old lace was indeed an effective marketing strategy. One wonders if these names were randomly applied and if anyone really knew the difference? Family legend also suggests that Lady Harriet visited

*Lady Harriet Kavanagh (reproduced by kind permission). Back of portrait reads: Mrs Harriet nee Le Poer Trench daughter of 2nd Earl of Clancarty, Married Thomas Kavanagh, 1825. Artist unknown.*

Venice and Milan and purchased specimens of Genoa tape lace. Although we cannot be sure where these examples were purchased, our comparisons of the family lace with the Borris lace and other designs in the collection are very confirming. Among the old family lace we have identified Milanese, Flemish, Maltese, Brussels appliqué on net, point de Gaze and Irish crochet.

## THE BORRIS LACE INDUSTRY

**Portraits of the** first patron of the Borris Lace Industry, Lady Harriet Kavanagh, and her successor, Mrs Frances Kavanagh, hang above the grand central staircase at Borris House.

*Frances Kavanagh, nee Forde Leithley. Artist unknown.*

in the account listings but their output was modest, most likely because they had young families and less time to spare.

When famine ravaged Ireland in 1847, women were found inspired with an energy to work that was truly inspiring. Whenever there was a female hand, it was set in motion, and, generally, it seized a needle, and wielded it vigorously for bread.[2]

The proof that Lady Harriet's exertions were wholly to relieve local poverty, not to bring profit to the estate, lies within the account records which show sale prices to be only a few pence above the price paid to the worker (see below). Sale prices would have had to cover the costs of posting the lace to dealers in London or directly to clients, of travelling to exhibitions and mounting the displays, as well as meeting the wages of the work mistress.

| Lace item | Price paid to workers | Price for sale |
| --- | --- | --- |
| Squares edged | 1s 8d | 2s 0d |
| No. 39 | 4s 6d | 5s 2d |

Small lace squares from pattern 1 (Catalogue item no. 1, Project 6) were given to beginners. Workers were paid 1 shilling for each 13 cm square. These squares were produced in large quantities and we found numerous patterns for them in the collection. For a square edged in needlelace, the worker received 1s 8d against a sale price of 2s 0d. Several of these squares were often inserted into tablecloths and pillow covers in chequerboard patterns.

The Borris Lace Industry was established in 1846 under the direction of Lady Harriet Kavanagh who drew the designs herself, having grown up in an age when all well-bred women studied art. Described as 'highly-gifted' and 'a woman of high culture and unusual artistic power', Lady Harriet modified the designs 'by her taste and skill to suit the fashion', then taught the women on the estate to work them.[1] Work was distributed each week to women from the poorest families. Older women produced most of the work. A few women in their twenties appear

*When famine ravaged Ireland in 1847, women were found inspired with an energy to work that was truly inspiring. Whenever there was a female hand, it was set in motion, and, generally, it seized a needle, and wielded it vigorously for bread. (Meredith, 1865)*

A large tablecloth, Catalogue item no. 70, is a typical example, and Borris lace items in the National Museum of Ireland include many of these squares.

For the deep border of Stock Sample 39 (see Sampler 2, p.44), the worker received 4s 6d per yard; it was sold at 5s 2d per yard. (The item numbers in the catalogue are a running sequence and do not match the lace sample numbers. Details of the original sample numbers are recorded in the notes column of the catalogue where known. Interestingly, if you check the notes for items 54 and 55 you see that no. 39 A and B had increased in price by 1912, the date of the fourth sampler) to 6s 9d.)

In 1855, Harriet's son Arthur married his cousin Frances Forde Leathley, a clergyman's daughter. Arthur had inherited the estate in February 1853 following the untimely deaths of his two older brothers. Arthur was born with only stumps for arms and legs yet managed to live a full and productive life. Known as 'the Cripple Kavanagh', he become a good horseman (with the aid of a special saddle), a fine fisherman, a fair shot and an intrepid traveller, could wield an axe and fell trees, produced seven healthy children — four sons and three daughters — and was elected to the British House of Commons in 1856 (Ireland at this time belonged to Britain). Arthur worked tirelessly for the improvement of his estates and the welfare of his people. 'He replaced at a merely nominal rent the tumble-down thatched cottages by others, roomy, well-slated, and comfortable. He himself drew the plans, and received a medal of the Royal Dublin Society for the best cottage at the lowest cost'.[3] This was at a time when 40 per cent of the houses in Ireland were one-room mud cabins with mud floors and neither windows nor chimney, so that the smoke from the fire escaped through the open door.[4] The township of Borris prospered from the sawmill that Arthur established and he also instigated the building of the graceful 16-arch viaduct, situated just below the town, which carried the (now defunct) Great Southern and Western Railway line between Bagenalstown and Wexford. It was said that Arthur succeeded in everything he attempted and that he had an 'engaging manner, so genial, so manly and so full of sympathy'.[5] He was loved by his tenantry and is reputed to have found outlets for Borris lace on his trips to London while in Parliament. Frances's devotion to Arthur gives us an indication of her own strength of character.

Frances took over the management of the lace industry after her marriage to Arthur and from all accounts she was just as capable and earnest as her mother-in-law. 'All of this was … taken up by Mrs Kavanagh [who] by her unwearied superintendence brought [it] to such perfection that "Borris lace" soon became well known for its beautiful designs and delicate workmanship, not surpassed in its own style by any of the "cottage industries" of Ireland', wrote Sarah Steele, Arthur's cousin, in a biography published in 1891, not long after his death.[6] The reference to 'cottage industries is interesting, appearing to indicate the existence of other tape lace cottage industries (such as the one at Ardee in County Louth), although we have found no references to others from this period.

The quality of the lace the workers produced would have depended not only on their abilities and their insights, but also on the sound direction supplied by Lady Harriet and Frances, and the good taste and intelligence of the work mistresses. Frances extended the Borris lacemaking industry by holding weekly classes, first in the Protestant School and later in the cottages. Training in lacemaking in nineteenth century Ireland was traditionally given free of charge.[7] Materials were distributed in class and beginners were started on small squares. Frances's standards were high and legend has it that she was quick to take the scissors to any work that was carelessly made. The offenders bemoaned these actions, but one can understand that Frances was seeking to maintain a standard of excellence.

*Frances extended the Borris lacemaking industry by holding weekly classes, first in the Protestant School and later in the cottages.*

A number of women from the township of Ballyragget in County Kilkenny, some 35 kilometres (21miles) distant, which formed part of another of the Kavanagh estates and was the location of a Georgian lodge to which Lady Harriet moved after Arthur's marriage, also made Borris lace.[8] It is testament to Lady Harriet's energy and drive that she promoted lacemaking to the women on the Ballyragget estate, where she lived until her death in 1885. On the day of her funeral all businesses in Borris closed. There was an overwhelming attendance of the tenantry and display of love and honour from those 'who came within the sphere of her refining influence [and] tears of those she befriended in the dark hours of desolation and poverty'.[9]

Sponsorship of the Borris lace industry was a responsibility passed down to each new mistress of the estate – from Lady Harriet Kavanagh to Mrs Frances Kavanagh, Mrs Helen Kavanagh and Mrs Mina Alice McMurrough Kavanagh – until it finally closed in the 1960s. Each in her turn employed work mistresses. In 1872, a Mrs Poole was paid £12 per year, with one penny to the pound commission, which raised her annual salary to between £32 and £36 per year. Miss Rebecca Devine, Mrs Purdy and Mrs Jacob followed Mrs Poole.[10] The last instructor to be employed was a Miss Christine Alexander of Milford, County Carlow, who travelled to Borris by train each week to conduct a lace class.[11] This must have been before 1931, when the railway line was closed to passenger traffic. (The Alexanders were related to the Kavanaghs through Mrs C.F. 'Fanny' Alexander, a well-known hymn-writer, whose son married Arthur Kavanagh's eldest daughter, Eva Francis.) The task of the work mistress was the independent management of the trade in lace, which included: 'the giving out and receiving the lace, drawing patterns for it, correspondence respecting orders and account keeping [and] firmness and strictness with the workers'.[12] Mrs May King, described as a supervisor in the 1930s and 1940s, was responsible for laundering the items for sale and may not have been involved in book-keeping duties.[13]

Orders for lace such as this were received from wealthy patrons in Ireland and England:

April 1914, the Hon. Lady Littleton, Government House, Royal Hospital, Chelsea, London S.W. Fichu no. 2. 10/6

There were also large orders from America and the Continent.

Orders were received for pillow covers, sheet edges, collars, table sets, table cloths, d'oyleys, blouses and nightdress bodices, blouse inserts, dress front, flounces and edgings. When the standard of design and workmanship was at its height, in the early years of the industry, from 1855 to 1870, between twenty and forty lacemakers were kept in employment, the best among them earning £400–£600 a year. By 1907 only fourteen workers remained. There was still a 'ready market, but no more labour [was] available' (presumably due to emigration and increasing industrialisation).[14] The shortage of lacemakers was unfortunate, coinciding as it did with a period when wearing handmade Irish lace became a national cause. Lady Aberdeen, for example, held a very successful vice-regal ball at Dublin Castle and insisted as an entry requirement that both men and women wear some form of Irish lace.

After the First World War, demand for handmade lace declined due to the competition from cheaper mass-produced machine-made lace. The cost of materials had risen and factory wages were higher, making it more difficult to find willing lacemakers. After 1919 the bulk of the orders came from

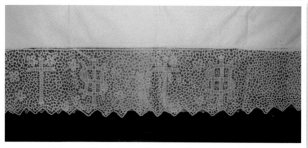

*Altar fall of Borris lace on the altar of the Sacred Heart Catholic Church, Borris*

the Irish Linen Stores in London.

In the 1930s Father Murphy, parish priest of Borris, tried to revive demand by organising Borris lace exhibitions in Dublin. For some time he was successful, obtaining sufficient orders to keep the few remaining lacemakers employed. In 1936, an altar fall made by a Mrs King won the Irish Countrywomen's Association Prize. It is still used in the old granite Sacred Heart Catholic Church in the main street of Borris. Father John proudly showed it to us, explaining that it is cherished by the congregation and only used on special occasions. A wide lace panel backed in red satin, which shows off the lace to good effect, features the crag design with insertions of shamrocks and religious motifs. The vandyked edging is similar to catalogue item number 13 (see photo 43 on page p.48).

Between 1910 and 1930 the lace was mainly used for trimming undergarments or for collars and cuffs. By 1930 when these items ceased to be fashionable the workers focused on producing table mats in various shapes and sizes.[15] The industry seems to have remained reasonably productive into the 1930s, for *The Times* of 19 October 1936 reported that at the marriage of Lord Kildare and Miss McMurrough Kavanagh all nine attendants wore collars and cuffs of Borris lace on their velvet dresses.

Changing fashions and the hardships of the Second World War resulted in a decline in demand for Borris lace, as indeed for all European laces. Additionally, the destruction of the Belgian lace factories and the reduction of output from the Nottingham factories meant that tape was difficult to obtain. In 1941, after much correspondence, S.A. Sands & Sons, Lace and Net Manufacturers of Nottingham, supplied some tape to the Borris Lace Industry, but it was of inferior quality and the first orders were not able to be used. A letter from the company dated 29 November 1941 reads in part: 're order for braids, delay due to them having to be made … I am having to do work of national importance in addition to keeping my lace business going'. After the war, machine-made tape was again bought in wholesale quantities by the Borris industry.

The numerous lace manufacturing ventures in Ireland were not equally successful. Despite periods of difficulty, the better managed ones continued to produce lace in fluctuating quantities into the twentieth century.[16] The degree of success reflected the energy of the patron and the influence of the connections through whom sales of the products could be made.[17] Well-connected society ladies could obtain high prices for all of the work their dependants could produce. Borris lace was a well-managed enterprise which continued into the 1960s, by which time there were only six lacemakers left in the village and most of their work was exported to America.

## BALLANTRAE LACE INDUSTRY

**The success of** the Borris venture is reflected in the fact that in 1908 it was extended to include a tandem enterprise at Glenapp Castle in Ballantrae, Scotland. Ballantrae is on the coast of Carrick in South Ayrshire. It was uncommon for such charitable enterprises to extend further than their locality or to develop larger networks of operation.[1] Records at Borris House reveal that patterns were sent from Borris with a teacher to instruct the Scottish workers. The facilitator of this arrangement was Mrs May Stock, of Glenapp Castle, second daughter of Frances Kavanagh. May Stock must have been involved with her mother in managing the Borris Lace Industry prior to her marriage, to have enabled her to set up such a closely duplicated enterprise. The portrait of May Stock hangs above the stairs in Borris House.

Items identical to some of those in the Borris Collection, but labelled Ballantrae lace, are held in the Glasgow Museum.[2] Pattern

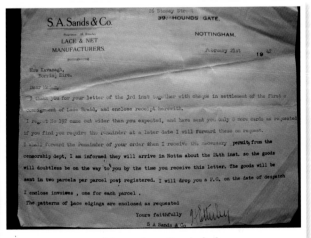

*1942 letter from Sands & Co.*

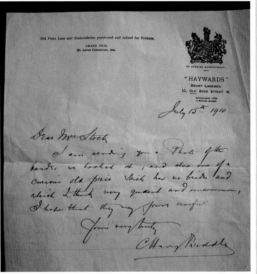

*Above: May Stock, founder of the Ballantrae lace industry, as a young woman. Portrait by Hubert Herkomer. Top right: A pattern marked 'Patterns & lace samples of these taken to Ballantrae June 2.' Bottom right: Letter to May Stock from Haywards, London*

names like net and crag appear, as in Borris lace, and Ballantrae lace is identical in every detail of design and stitch technique. The stationery used by the Ballantrae Lace Industry was identical in design to that used in Borris. The Ballantrae business card reads: 'Ballantrae Lace Industry, Orders received by Mrs Henry Stock, Glenapp Castle, Ballantrae, N.B.' (N.B. means North Britain, as Scotland was referred to in the early twentieth century.) Finished articles were sold in Glasgow and London.[3]

Account books at Borris House record transactions involving the sending of patterns and materials to Ballantrae, for example, 'Box

of Braid 30 pieces, 180 yds to Ballantrae post 6d'. There is also a pattern with the notation: 'Patterns & lace samples of these taken to Ballantrae June 2.'

Further evidence of the connection between Borris and Ballantrae is provided in a letter found in the records at Borris House. The letter, from Haywards to May Stock, dated 1910, discusses the forwarding of patterns 'very quaint and uncommon'. It was a common practice for large marketing firms in London like Haywards and Girvans to send patterns with orders.[4]

A curious entry in *The Times* of 17 March

1911 reported on the sale of home industries at the home of the Marchioness of Waterford in London, which included work from 'Mrs Stock's Borris Lace Industry'. This is the only reference we have found to Mrs Stock and Borris lace rather than Ballantrae lace.

May's husband, James Henry Stock MP, died in 1907, before the commencement of the Ballantrae Lace Industry. Glenapp Castle was sold in 1917 and May Stock moved back to Borris, where she remained for the remainder of her life (d. 1949). Mrs Inglis, the local bank manager's wife, carried on the business after May left until around 1920, when lacemaking ceased.[5] No other industry records or account books from Ballantrae were found at Borris House. The present members of the Kavanagh family were unaware of the establishment of a tandem lace industry in Ballantrae, although they knew of May Stock's connections with Scotland.

## WHO WERE THE BORRIS LACEMAKERS?

❧ **Irish lacemakers have** been described as patient, painstaking, diligent, intelligent, possessing great manual dexterity and they did not 'shrink from' any amount of 'trouble or expenditure of time'.[1] Yet these Irishwomen were from the poorer classes and their lives were extremely hard, eking out a most meagre livelihood. Lacemaking endowed thousands of homes around Ireland with a means of employment, perhaps bringing some small comforts but most of all mental elevation. A skilled worker could engage her fancy in the way that she executed the designs to produce artistic beauty and without wandering from the sanctuary of her home.[2] Although income from lacemaking was modest, it could make a valuable contribution to the family income. In small country villages like Borris, there would have been few other employment openings for women.

In Borris, a unique lace was produced, workers were paid a fair, set price and orders sought and filled. Emily Jackson made the important observation that:

> the cost of tools and working materials is so trifling that the profit is derived almost entirely from the manual labour expended upon it, and the scope for artistic feeling and individuality in the taste of the worker is so great that a very high value can be obtained by the humblest operator.[3]

Unfortunately, handmade lace was seldom signed so its creators remain anonymous. At best, handmade laces 'emanate something of the maker whose fingers created them'.[4] Records in the Borris Lace Collection, mostly loose sheets of paper, list the lacemakers' names, often with their ages and the work they were presenting for payment.

Some workers were much more prolific than others, probably due to their age and experience. Historically, lacemakers were trained from a very young age but we have no evidence to suggest that young children were trained at Borris. Perhaps this was because there was no lace school on the estate, just weekly classes.

We also have no idea as to the identity of the originators of Borris Lace. There are no photos in the collection or at Borris House and we

| LACE | PRICE | NAME OF WORKER | AGE |
|---|---|---|---|
| Cushion no. 1 | 23/6, 25/6 | Bridget Walshe | 50 |
| Cushion no. 2 | 23/6, 25/- | Bridget Walshe | 50 |
| Cushion no. 3 | 25/-, 26/6 | Mrs Flanagan | 39 |
| Cushion no. 4 | 25/-, 26/6 | Mrs King | 44 |
| Cushion no. 5 | 25/-, 26/6 | Mrs Connelly | 70 |
| Cushion no. 6 | 23/6, 25/- | Mrs Egan | 72 |
| 6 fine d'oyleys | 10/6, 11/6 | Mrs Summers | 41 |
| 4 dinner mats | 10/-, 11/- | Nellie Byrne | 21 |
| 1 table centre | £2.12/6, £2.15/6 | Mrs Egan | 72 |
| 6 rounds | 2/6, 3/- | Mrs Breen | 25 |
| 12 squares: 6 net, 6 crag | 2/6, 3/8 | Mrs Breen | 25 |
| 6 yds no. 36 | £1.5/-, £1.6/6 | Mrs Nolan | 61 |
| 6 yds no. 42 insertion | 8/6, 9/9 | Mrs King | 44 |
| 6 yds no. 42 edging | 9/- | Mrs King | 44 |
| 6 yds no. 40 edging | 9/- | May Fennell | 20 |
| 1 sofa spread | £1.7/6, £1.9/6 | Mrs Connely | 70 |

have not found any other photos of lacemakers despite extensive inquiries in the district.

We do have some names, however, written on a page of telegram stationery from Glenapp Castle. We assume that the undated list relates to workers at Borris, as it was found with the Borris Lace Industry account books.

The lacemakers range from 20 to 72 years of age. May Fennell, listed above, married and became Mrs May King, Borris lace supervisor.[5] Lace edging was produced by the yard and paid, according to the design (width), from 4 shillings to £1 per yard. Six-yard lengths were a common order, possibly for edging tablecloths, bed sheets and crinoline skirts. Borris workers earned on average 8 pence a day, which was not unreasonable for part-time employment in

that era.[6] In 1893, an article in *The Economic Journal* on the survival of domestic industries described the part-time nature of lacemaking: 'much is done in the intervals of time otherwise filled up'.[7] In good times the Borris Lace Industry turned over about £600 a year.

It was most important that the lace be kept perfectly clean, and the workers became known for their cleanliness both in person and in their homes in contrast to the normal standards of the day.[8] It is easy to imagine that they preferred to make lace in their own homes and in essence work for themselves rather than work as servant for a master. Borris lace in particular provided plenty of scope for creative interpretation of the designs and choice of stitch placement, which 'puts the lace-worker on a superior footing to the woman who merely works a machine' or works for a master.[9] In addition, the work could easily be done by women in delicate health.

Some employers, however, lamented the loss to lacemaking of embroidery, mending and dressmaking skills, which were a very necessary accomplishment for servant girls:

> Increased rates of wages failed to induce them to become servants, as long as they could procure any sort of living by needlework: and a strong tendency to neglect the useful application of the art of sewing, in the desire to pursue the ornamental, prevailed very extensively.[10]

Mrs Greta Carter, born in 1921, is the last of the Borris lacemakers. Until recently she lived in one of the pretty low-ceilinged cottages standing one against the other at the top of the main street, and built originally by Arthur Kavanagh for his estate workers. Mrs Carter learnt to make Borris lace in the 1930s from her aunt, Mrs May King, one of the industry's supervisors. Greta's father was the bailiff on the Borris estate and her mother worked in the house itself; as Greta explained, 'If you got in there you were safe'.[11]

In later years another Mrs King became a leading exponent of Borris lace after her retirement as Carlow Library's branch librarian, and in 1960 had two students of Borris lace under her careful supervision. We know that she won ICA-sponsored prizes for a set of placemats and an altar fall, so her work must have been of a high standard. Mrs King was taught lacemaking from the age of twelve by her grandmother, who was a well-known Borris lacemaker.[12]

## THE ICA REVIVAL OF IRISH LACE

❧ **The Irish Countrywomen's** Association (ICA), founded in 1910, is the largest women's organisation in Ireland. It has been responsible, with mixed success, for several attempts at reviving waning or lost forms of Irish lace. In 1959 the ICA sponsored an inter-federation competition to help encourage the few lacemakers who were trying to revive Borris lace. At the time the lacemakers had considerable difficulty in obtaining the fine tape needed to reproduce the old patterns.

Much later, in 1991, when some members of the ICA Carlow Federation decided to revive the forgotten art of Borris lace, they sought the help of Faith Green, a Branscombe lace teacher from Plymouth in England who had some experience of Borris lace. Faith Green had been one of the participants in the Borris lace class at the English Lace School at Rockbeare in Devon, conducted by Mrs Corrigan from Borris some years earlier. It is a little sad and ironic that by 1991 there were no Borris lacemakers in Ireland able to help bring about the revival.

A November 1991 article in the *National & Leinster Times* with the headline 'Borris Lace: No Longer a Dying Art', included a photograph of Faith Green teaching a group of ICA Carlow Federation women, among them Ena Atkinson. Shortly afterwards an article about Borris lace by Faith Green (1992) appeared in the (English) Guild of Needle Laces journal, with accompanying photographs.[1] The items shown in the photographs are not, however, comparable to the pieces in the collection at Borris House. These and other more recently worked examples of Borris lace, although using the old designs, not surprisingly appear to reflect Branscombe lace techniques. New stitches and design concepts have been introduced which demonstrate the maker's creativity and knowledge of Branscombe stitches but do not reflect a considered study of Borris lace. This is understandable, given that the lace at Borris House has never been on permanent public display. Patterns were given to Faith Green when she visited Borris, but they involve only a single design line with no indication of stitches. Branscombe lace is undoubtedly the closest relation to Borris lace, but the techniques have some defining differences, summarised in table of comparisons on page 42.

It appears that tape lace was not successfully taken up elsewhere in Ireland, so once the Borris Lace Industry ended there was no knowledge of the general techniques to refer to and no recorded instruction. Ena Atkinson was the only one from the class with Faith Green who continued to work the lace and has been tireless in trying to revive interest through exhibitions, magazine articles, demonstrating and teaching. Recommended to us as the person most knowledgeable about Borris lace, Ena's workmanship and designs are inspiring, and it was a pleasure to study the lace with her, discuss techniques and history, and share our stories. Despite her dedication, Borris lace has not seen a revival and has not been taken up by anyone in County Carlow. Ena Atkinson

and Mary Sheil, a member of the Cork Lacemakers, joined us at Borris House for two days while we were in the early stages of cataloguing. This was their first opportunity to study the lace, and at that stage we were all still under the impression that the stitches used were the familiar and classic stitches of needlelace.

In 1991 the Guild of Irish Lacemakers organised an exhibition in Dublin to coincide with Celebrating Dublin 1991, a European City of Culture event. The exhibition was titled 'Irish Airs and Laces: An Exhibition of Lace'. A section of the catalogue was devoted to Borris lace, providing a summarised history of the industry and descriptions of three items. One of the pieces was unfinished, all were labelled antique. While most of the other laces listed in the catalogue were contemporary, for Borris lace only antique items were available, a telling sign that it was in need of revival.

*It appears that tape lace was not successfully taken up elsewhere in Ireland, so once the Borris Lace Industry ended there was no knowledge of the general techniques to refer to and no recorded instruction.*

The Cork Lacemakers have included Borris lace in their study course of Irish laces. Instruction is available but, once again, the designs and worked examples on close inspection are not consistent with the lace in the Borris Lace Collection. We feel this comment is relevant due to the comprehensiveness of the original collection and the fact that it is original and not recently assembled.

## WHY IS BORRIS LACE SO LITTLE KNOWN?

↜ **In 1873 Mrs** Bury Palliser, at the end of a long listing of the laces made in the different locations around Ireland at the time of the Great Famine, finished with 'and various other descriptions of lace of admirable finish'.[1] Were there just too many to mention or was she afraid of missing the more obscure? It is a regular occurrence that in each classic study of Irish laces the well known are carefully documented, but Borris lace does not receive a mention. It has been overlooked and undocumented despite the fact that it was commercially produced for over one hundred years. A 1960 article republished in the *English Lace School Newsletter* affirms our belief that

*The Kavanaghs were Protestant, and perhaps the family and the lace industry they sponsored were to some degree shunned and set apart in a decidedly Catholic Ireland. It seems curious that the Irish laces which have become the best known are those which were taught in Catholic-run lace schools.*

Borris lace, 'another Irish needlepoint of the later nineteenth century, although produced on a small scale and less ambitious in designs and technique, deserves to be better known to the public'.[2] Admittedly, production of Borris lace was always on a smaller scale than the well-known laces like Irish crochet, Limerick and Carrickmacross. In a 1971 listing of principal Irish laces, Borris lace was again not included.[3] In contrast to the thousands of women reported as occupied in the production of Irish crochet, 1500 employed in making Limerick lace and 120 workers of Youghal lace, the highest number of recorded workers of Borris lace was around forty. The Borris Lace Industry was said to have started with about twenty elderly widows who were in special need.[4] The undated listing on page 25 shows only twelve productive lacemakers; a listing from 1907 showed fourteen. Nevertheless, the Borris Lace Industry remained commercially viable until well into the twentieth century.

A possible explanation for the lack of attention afforded Borris lace might be that 'philanthropic effort was organised on distinct religious grounds and this proved to be both a cohesive and divisive force in regard to those institutions established by women'.[5] In many situations, nuns taught lacemaking and organised distribution within religious orders. Alternatively, we see patrons from landed estates setting up their own enterprises. It is possible that many of these patrons were Catholic and able to work alongside the nuns and their convent enterprises. The Kavanaghs, however were Protestant, and perhaps the family and the lace industry they sponsored were to some degree shunned and set apart in a decidedly Catholic Ireland. It seems curious that the Irish laces which have become the best known are those which were taught in Catholic-run lace schools.

Although the Borris lace cottage industry operated from 1846 until the 1960s, the lace itself is rarely discovered, even in museums within Ireland. The Dublin Museum has several small items, including a framed gift of lace presented to Irish President Cearbhall O'Dalaigh by the Kavanagh family in 1975. The most interesting piece is the cuff dated 1868, mentioned earlier. A square muslin-centred handkerchief (Object number DT: 1967.41) is labelled 'Borris lace', but none of the fillings or picots in this piece are characteristic of the lace in the Borris Lace Collection.

Apart from the altar fall in the Catholic Church in Borris, the only other items that we have discovered are privately owned. Bobby Smith of Lorum, County Carlow, has a blouse with Borris lace inserts and a d'oyley similar to pieces in the collection. We have not yet discovered any items of Borris lace in collections in Australia. A skirt front labelled 'Branscombe lace with holly point fillings' sold recently on eBay came from a collector in England — it was, however, a classic and very nice example of Borris lace. Perhaps Borris lace is not so rare, but is not easily identified due to the lack of published information.

Design quality was obviously a problem with Borris lace, as indeed it was with many of the Irish laces of the period. That Irish lace was 'uncouth in pattern', which 'militates against its successful sale', was a constant cry according to *The Times* in 1885. Disappointing design prompted Alan Cole from the South Kensington Museum to visit Ireland in 1883 to urge designers and makers of Irish lace to introduce new and improved design to their work. Frances Kavanagh was obviously aware of this, for although there is no mention of Borris lace in Cole's lengthy article 'Renascence of the Irish Art of Lace-

NEW PATTERNS FOR IRISH LACE.

The endeavour to obtain new patterns for the use of Irish lace-makers was commenced in 1884, under the patronage of a Committee which since then has been added to. This Committee at present consists of the following:

Her Excellency the Marchioness of Londonderry.
The Duke of Devonshire, K.G.
The Duchess of St. Albans.
The Duchess of Wellington.
Lady Dorothy Nevill.
The Earl Spencer, K.G.
The Countess Spencer.
The Countess of Aberdeen.
The Earl Rosse.
The Viscount Monck.
The Lord Emly.
The Lord Carlingford, K.P.
The Lord Monteagle.
The Lady O'Hagan.
Sir Richard Wallace, Bart., K.C.B., M.P.
Sir George and Lady Colthurst.
The Dowager Lady Colthurst.
The Hon. Mrs. Pereira.
The Hon. Mrs. Albert Petre.
Mrs. Alfred Morrison.
The Hon. Mr. Justice O'Hagan.
The Hon. Mrs. O'Hagan.
The Drapers' Company.
The Skinners' Company.
Mrs. Adair.
J. T. Brunner, Esq., M.P.
Miss Keane.
Colonel and Mrs. Donnelly.
Mrs. Power Lalor.
Richard Bagwell, Esq.
Mrs. Alan Cole.
Vere Foster, Esq.
W. E. H. Lecky, Esq.
Mrs. Arthur Kavanagh.
E. Falconer Litton, Esq., Q.C.
Edward W. O'Brien, Esq.
Mrs. R. Vere O'Brien.
Mrs. Arthur Trench.
John E. Vernon, Esq.

*List of Committee Members who contributed to a fund to offer prizes for new patterns for the use of Irish lacemakers. Mrs Arthur Kavanagh contributed the sum of £2 (from Cole 1888).*

making',[6] she is listed as one of thirty-nine distinguished patrons of a Committee of Review in 1884 that endeavoured to obtain new patterns for the use of Irish lacemakers to improve their designs. Frances subscribed the sum of £2, the figure set for patrons of small industries, which went towards money prizes for design competitions. In 1885, forty-nine prizes were awarded among the 300 designs submitted. The working drawings from the competition were to be supplied directly to the laceworkers. Of these awards, three were important designs for albs, to be executed in cut linen or tape lace work, and eighteen were for 'furniture trimmings' to be carried out in tape lace,[7] so it would seem that Mrs Kavanagh's subscription was well invested.

Alan Cole summed up the general situation as follows:

> The making of lace in Ireland is a domestic industry practiced by some hundreds of peasants in their homes, by communities in convents, by children in industrial and other schools and by others. Great skill in the work has been developed since the earlier part of the present century when the industry was introduced to the country through the efforts of philanthropists BUT the development of this skill has not been accompanied with the production and use of well designed patterns.[8]

A report written by Alan Cole a year earlier details his visits to Irish lacemaking and embroidery schools. The Garryhill Embroidery Industry seems to have been set up in a very similar way to the Borris Lace Industry.

> Garryhill Embroidery Industry established by Lady Duncannon and [is] under her direction. The industry is carried on in cottages, and I visited seven of them, seeing the work in progress under the hands of two or three workers in each cottage.
>
> The system under which the management of the industry is organised is as follows: Lady Duncannon and her Manager in London cause all the designs for the workers' use to be prepared and transferred to the linen. The agent on the spot pays the workers for work done ... thoroughly business-like and practical ... leading to a just appreciation of the industry as a real business that depends upon their best efforts to turn out good work and to profit by the direction and instruction given to them.[9]

Cole also visited the Presentation Convent at Kilkenny and the Waterford School of Art (which he noted shared designs with the workers at New Ross). The Convents of Mercy at Clonakilty and at Ennis, Kinsale and others were also mentioned. Not all were lace schools and some were small scale. Cole reported modest progress taking place at Innishmacsaint, Coppoquin, Newtonbarrry and Borris, 'where ladies supervise the work of small groups of peasant women'.[10] Cole does not say he visited Borris, but at least he was aware of the enterprise. He may have had a snobbish contempt for Borris lace simply because it was a tape lace, for tape laces were often denounced as crude and inferior.

Historian Nicola Bowe (1989) confirms that 'rural, philanthropic ventures were overlooked by Cole and the Arts and Crafts movement in Ireland and attention was paid to Lace schools and especially those attached to art schools'.[11]

Borris lace was never affiliated with a design school or designers nor, it seems, did it ever receive an award at the national or international level. Prizes at the International Exhibitions so popular in the nineteenth century did much to elevate the respective laces by way of fostering important commissions and demand generally. Admittedly, Borris lace was less ambitious in design and technique than many other laces, and was not comparable to the design and workmanship of the Youghal and Kenmare laces of the period.

Lady Harriet's venture was not unique, as numerous cottage-based industries flourished in Scotland, Wales and Ireland during the latter half of the nineteenth century[12], and while many such enterprises are covered in the literature in some detail there is no mention of Borris lace.

Lady Aberdeen, wife of the Irish viceroy, was chiefly responsible for the setting up of the Irish Home Industries Association. Its purpose was to unite and assist all the isolated cottage and home industries by providing connections to those anxious to purchase their work. It was also charged with raising the awareness of Irish goods and 'getting up a reputation for them'.[13] Lady Aberdeen mostly achieved this through Irish Industries Exhibitions and Sales which were usually held in the grand homes of London society. Members of the royal family frequently attended and made large purchases; all of this was reported by *The Times* in fullest detail. Exhibition catalogues include Irish tape laces in the 1850s and 1860s,[14] and again in 1883, 1885 and 1886. Although we cannot be sure if the laces were from Borris or Ardee, by 1883 it was reported that Ardee lace had degenerated to the point where it was of little market value.[15]

**EXHIBITIONS AND SALES OF IRISH INDUSTRIES WHICH INCLUDED A STAND FOR BORRIS LACE**

|  |  |
|---|---|
| 1883 | Irish Industries Exhibition and Sale, The Mansion House, London.[16] |
| 1892 | Irish Cottage Industries Sale, Londonderry House, London. |
| 1898 | Irish Textile Exhibition, Royal University Buildings, Dublin.[17] |
| 1905 | Dublin Horse Show, Dublin. |
| 1907 | Irish International Exhibition in Dublin.[18] |
| 1909 | St Patrick's Day Exhibition at Devonshire House, London. |
| 1911 | Royal Irish Industries Sale, Lansdowne House, London. |
| 1911 | Home Industries Sale, London. |
| 1913 | Irish Industries Association Exhibition and Sale, Londonderry House, London. |
| 1913 | Royal Dublin Society's Art Exhibition.[19] |

The following list, compiled mostly from articles in *The Times*, details a consistent presence of Borris lace in the marketplace despite the small scale manufacture.

Like other Irish laces, Borris lace received royal patronage. Faith Green reports that Borris lace 'was presented to Queen Victoria and later many members of the Royal Family wore the lace'.[20] While we have not been able substantiate this claim it is possible that the information came from Mrs Corrigan of Borris who is known to have been very knowledgeable on the subject. Older members of the Kavanagh family remember that a large order came through from Givens of London, about 1938, for a set of table mats for the English Royal Train for the tour of South Africa by the King and Queen. Mrs Carter of Borris recalled that due to the Kavanaghs' connections, many important commissions for items of Borris lace found their way to wedding ceremonies and stately homes as far away as Russia.[21]

The unique stitches and techniques which remained unrecorded ensured that Borris lace could not be easily copied or reproduced accurately outside the carefully

*The unique stitches and techniques which remained unrecorded ensured that Borris lace could not be easily copied or reproduced accurately outside the carefully managed industry. While possibly deliberate, this most certainly contributed to the lace almost becoming extinct and forgotten.*

managed industry. While possibly deliberate, this most certainly contributed to the lace almost becoming extinct and forgotten. In the early period at least, it may not have been practicable to record the stitch techniques. Few workers could copy patterns from written instructions but had no difficulty copying finished pieces.[22] Frances Kavanagh taught the workers herself in weekly classes and various work mistresses were employed. The women would also have taught each other, friends sharing their knowledge within the village circle and mothers teaching their daughters, as passing on their skills brought with it the ability to earn an income. Later, when the lace became uneconomical to produce, it was left to just a few culturally minded exponents to keep the knowledge alive. Sadly and inevitably much of the memory and detail has been lost.

A few brief articles appeared in lace magazines in the 1980s and 1990s, written mostly in response to Marie's efforts to share her discovery. Pat Earnshaw includes Borris on a map of lacemaking centres in Ireland, but a page on Irish tape laces has only a paragraph on Borris lace.[23]

A photograph in another of her books shows a piece of lace spilling from the bottom drawer of a chest; the design closely resembles the Borris crag lace in Project 12: Crag-edged hand towel.[24] The lace in the photograph is labelled 'Dichtl lace', an early twentieth century tape lace designed by German lacemaker Franziska Dichtl. This lace became popular throughout Europe and the name was later anglicised to Dickel.

The rarity of tape lace has obviously been a contributing factor in Borris lace not experiencing the revival seen with other Irish laces. Marie has been approached by lacemakers on several occasions during her regular visits to the country to show them how to use the tape, draw it up and start and finish the edges.

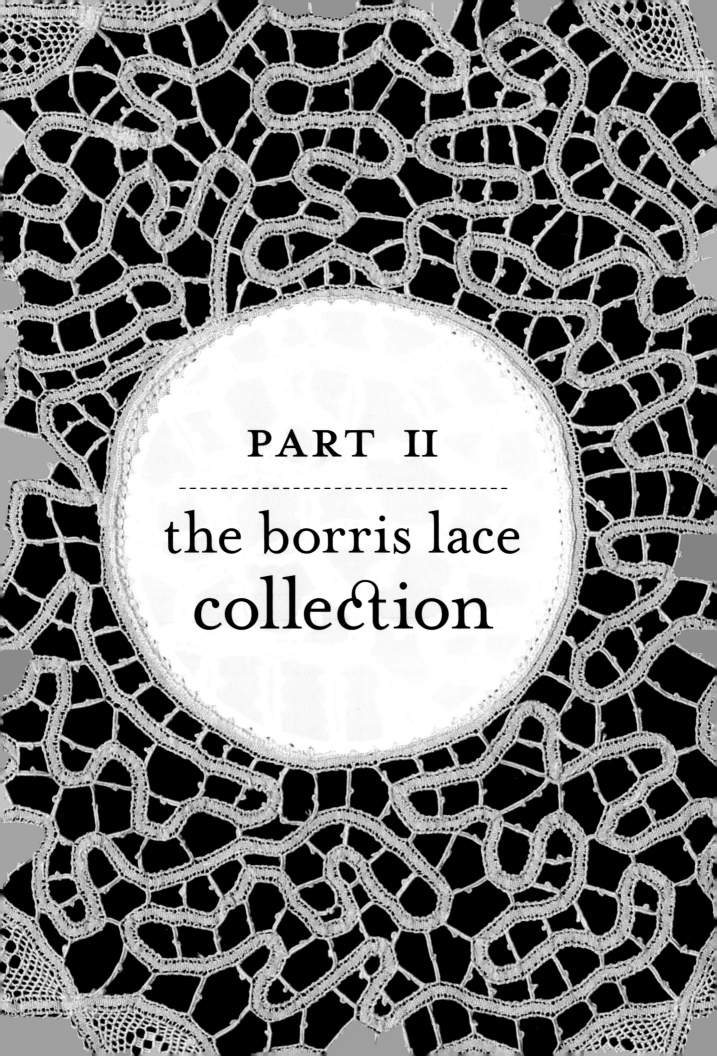

# PART II

----------------------------------------

## the borris lace
## collection

# The Borris Lace Collection is arguably one of the most complete collections of a lace industry to have survived in Ireland.

✙ **When lace schools** in Ireland closed, many of the records and patterns were lost or sold off to eager international buyers. The Borris Lace Collection includes family lace collected from travels abroad, which most probably provided the inspiration for Borris lace itself, and a number of items of old household linen, much of which is trimmed with Borris lace. When the Borris Lace Industry folded in the 1960s all the unsold stock and records were packed away into cardboard boxes, stored under beds and forgotten but preserved. Some of the unsold items reveal an amateurish quality. It is understandable that the best work sold quickly. Other loose items probably belonged to the family, as many show signs of wear. They include insertions, edgings, centrepieces and d'oyleys.

When we arrived to start our cataloguing, we found all the items wrapped in tissue paper. Everything was stored together – lace, thread, patterns, tapes, account books and other paper work.

We catalogued the entire collection of seventy-two individual items, as well as the family lace. Starting with the small d'oyleys we measured and photographed, identified new or unusual characteristics, sometimes under magnification, and recorded the details into a purpose built database using Microsoft Access. High-definition digital images provide a visual record of all items including ephemera. All items are now safely stored in archival mounts or in acid-free tissue, which was used to roll and wrap some of the larger items. The smaller items were inserted into sleeves of inert conservation-grade clear plastic. Mrs Kavanagh was very pleased with the plastic sleeve arrangement as it allows the lace to be viewed and handled without damage or soiling. It also expedites the processes of displaying and packing away.

## HOUSEHOLD LINEN

✙ **Linen items decorated** with Borris lace were collected from the household to be included in the catalogue. A heavy linen twill tape often used in the lace for household linen produced a hard-wearing lace which

*Catalogue item no. 69. A set of pillow covers of linen fabric with lace of linen twill braid. Lace edged on all sides 7.5 cm wide, gathered on corners. Opening is closed with handmade linen buttons and hand-stitched buttonholes.*

has survived well. Linen thread to match the weight of the linen tape was used to work the large net ground. Despite the heaviness, the lace is still very attractive. A K4 laundry mark, embroidered in red, appears on several items. The household linen is as grand as the house itself and includes a bedspread with lace panels, a bed sheet, pillow covers, tablecloths, table centres, placemats and d'oyleys.

A large and unusual linen tablecloth, for which the family is unable to ascribe a purpose, is made up of squares of variations of the no. 1 design with alternate hemstitched linen inserts. It has a large hole in the centre which is edged in Borris lace and appears to have been designed to stand up around some object. It is catalogued as item no. 70. Variations of tapes, interpretations and workmanship between the various squares indicate that they were worked by different lacemakers. Chequerboard tablecloths of alternating squares of lace and linen were mentioned in The Times in 1909 as a 'novelty'.

## CLOTHING

✢ **Items of clothing** include two Edwardian-style blouses with lace insertions, collars, cuffs and a dress-front. The account books record many orders for blouses in three designs. We were able to identify the two in the collection as designs 1 and 2. We also discovered many patterns for the lace edgings, collar and cuff insertions for these blouses, which both feature a wide foldback collar and a wide jabot falling from the neckline. The sleeves are fitted and gathered at the wrist with a frill extending

*Edwardian blouse no. 1 bears the laundry mark* 'STOCK'. *The wide lace edging the collar and jabot, and the lace for the cuffs and frills at the wrist, is all of the same design. (See catalogue entry no. 64.)*

*Edwardian blouse no. 2; all insertions are of crag lace. (See catalogue entry no. 65.)*

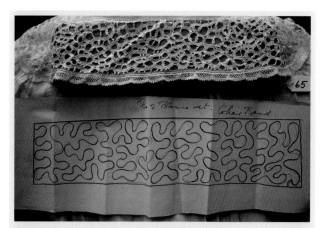

*Pattern for lace insert for blouse no. 2*

over the hand. The blouses are made of fine muslin, which shows off the lace to great effect, with a gathering at the waist centre back. Design 3 was more expensive, and presumably more elaborate, but unfortunately we found neither pattern nor lace samples. The blouses are accurately described in an article on Irish lace in *The Times* of 18 March 1909.

A 1912 order for blouse no. 1 reads: 'March 29, 1912 the Hon. Mrs Cahert, Adderley, Market Drayton, Salop. 1 no. 1 blouse 1.15.6p [£1 15s 6d]'.[1]

## FAMILY LACE

✌ **Items of family** lace in a variety of techniques are believed to have provided the inspiration and designs for the early Borris laces. A fabulous bobbin-made flounce of point de Milan was most likely the main influence. Two pieces of Flemish bobbin lace possibly provided the inspiration for the crag design. Other items of family lace include a magnificent point de Gaze full-length wedding veil, a large flounce of Brussels appliqué lace, Irish crochet and black Maltese bobbin lace.

## STOCK SAMPLERS

✌ **The collection includes** four large stock samplers (each 54 x 90 cm), of mounted lace specimens, which appear to represent the standard types of lace produced for over one hundred years. Each of the sixty-three stock samples was tagged with a Borris Lace Industry business card which included a pattern number and price, and occasionally the names of the stitches. These details match

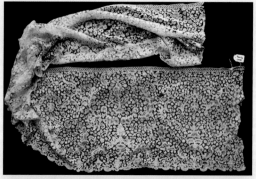
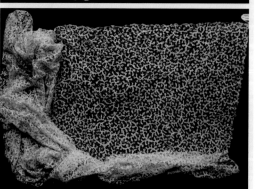

*Flemish bobbin lace flounce; flemish bobbin lace veil*

entries in the account books. The relative ages of the samplers are reflected in the condition and the degree of fading of the fabric of which they are made, in each case mauve satin backed with muslin. Stock Sampler 1 required careful stabilisation. Marie undertook this task and expertly drew the threads together with small running stitches.

Stock Sampler 1 is the oldest, and includes catalogue items nos 19 to 31. Stock Sampler 2 includes catalogue items

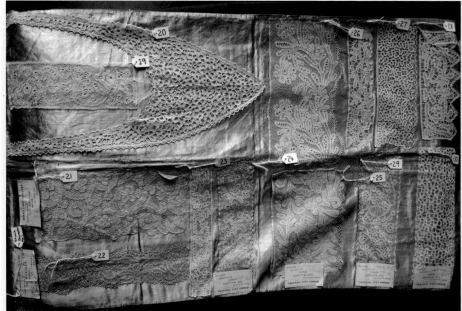

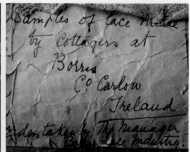

*Left: Stock Sampler 1
Above: Label on reverse of Stock
Sampler 2; the front of the
sampler appears on page 44
Below left: Stock Sampler 3
Below right: Stock Sampler 4*

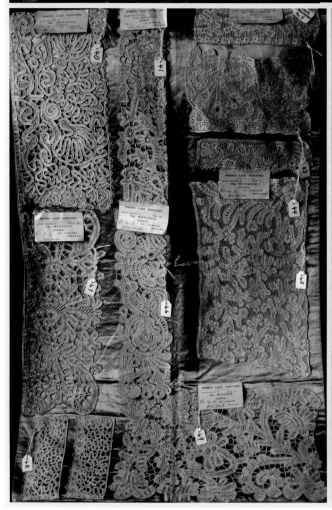

nos 32 to 39. It is also very faded but in fair condition. Most samples reflect the Milanese style, with sample no. 36 almost identical to the Milanese family lace. Stock Sampler 3 includes sample nos 40 to 49, which contain a wide variety of tapes and styles. Stock Sampler 4 is dark purple in colour, in good condition and obviously the most recent of the four. It includes sample nos 50 to 63. It is conveniently dated by sample no. 59, 'pattern of edging no. 40 Nov. 1912'. It also displays a newer version of the Borris Lace Industry business card.

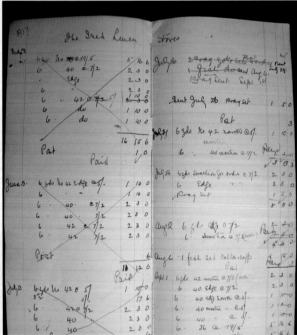

*Borris Lace Industry business cards and invoices; order book entries*

## BUSINESS RECORDS AND STATIONERY

**Account books, invoices,** letters, business cards and Borris Lace Industry letterhead add to the comprehensiveness of the collection.

The date 1846 is printed on the original invoices, some of which remain in the collection. Some more recent stationery bears the year 1857, and this has often been incorrectly taken as the starting date of the industry. We can, however, be sure of the 1846 start date, as it is documented that Frances took over the supervision of the well-established industry from Harriet after her marriage in 1855.

Account books survive from 1912 to 1930, and 1945 to September 1953, when recorded lace sales ceased. The books record the orders, the prices and the payments received. Private sales to friends and family connections in both England and Ireland were also common.

**Interesting entries from the Account Books 1912–1930**

- **July 12 1912**, 1 D'oyley fish 2/- sent to Mrs Stock, White Hall
- **November 25 1913**, Mrs Stock, 12 large dinner mats @ 6/9, 6 small with crag and net 4/6. (Mrs Stock, who was related to the Kavanagh family, placed regular orders.)
- **Dec 2 1913**, Mrs Maxwell, Hampton Court Palace, Middlesex. Collar 12/6 fine fish for Mrs Bates? (Mrs Bates may have been a favourite laceworker.)
- The Countess of Dudley, Witly Court, Worcester, 2 cushions 2.18.6 p
- **1913**, Marchioness of Winchester, 23

Cavendish Square, London W. 9 no. 37 mats @1/4. NOT PAID. (Goods were often sent on approval to private clients many of whom were often slow to pay despite reminders being sent. NOT PAID was not a rare entry.)

- **1915**, Mrs Kavanagh, Borris House, Borris. 2 cushions no.1 28" by 28". Returned.
- **July 25 1916**, Messrs Haywards, 11 Old Bond Street, London, W. 6 yds no 42 @5/- (Haywards were a regular purchaser until 1919 when Irish Linen Stores took over. In 1922 more orders from Haywards are listed.)
- **1916–1917** Fish pattern and crag edge were the most popular orders.
- **1919** The Irish Linen Stores, 112 New Bond St, London W. (Many orders were received and filled. This seems to be the beginning of the arrangement as the order book listed it in large letters. They remained the main supplier from this time. In one year sales mounted to £200. Monthly sales varied from £3 to £30.)
- **July 8** Fine lace for nightdress sent to Mrs Stock, The White Hall. £4/7/0
- **1926** Cami-knickers 'court' set £3/6/0 p (Cami-knickers were popular orders at this time, and expensive.)
- **1928** Shamrock 'doyles' design no. 34 (A popular order at this time along with nightdress tops)
- **1929** Most orders are from within Ireland and include names and addresses.
  It seems that orders are not being sent to London at this stage.
- **1930** Pomegranate design no. 8 (A popular order at this time yet very expensive.)

The invoice book covering 1945–1953 shows that business was slowing. The entries are mostly for private sales.

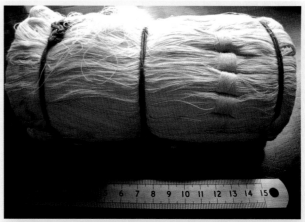

*Unused parcel of six slips of unbranded fine gassed cotton thread; unused tape from the collection*

## UNUSED MATERIALS

**One parcel of** a fine slip thread traditionally used by lacemakers is held in the collection. Slip thread came in long skeins (slips), each one wound separately and bundled into a figure of eight. The size of the thread was indicated by the number of slips in a parcel, held together by red twine or thread. The more slips, the finer the thread. Once the parcel was opened, the size information was lost. The parcel is a little disturbed but seems to contain six slips of fine gassed cotton thread, roughly equivalent to DMC

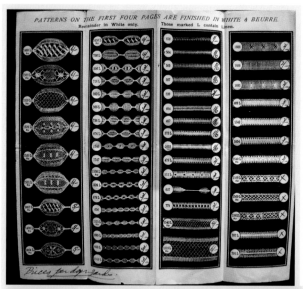

*One of several trade catalogues showing examples of Honiton and point lace braids with prices per dozen cards; design on pink glazed linen; pattern is well used*

Broder Machine no. 30 or Madeira Cotona 30. There are also a number of invoices for Barbours no. 60 Irish linen thread, but no unused thread remains.

There are several unused cards of tape, among them linen twill tape, silk tape and a wide variety of commercial tapes and edgings. Some of the older tape is very loosely woven.

All the tapes appear to be machine made.

In the braid catalogues in the collection a number of items are ticked: 564, 503, 3 dozen x 572, 576 (linen), 1730 and 1739. In a catalogue from Sands & Co. are two samples ticked for ordering: No. 486, a very fine braid, and No. 167, not so fine. Many of the cards of tape are labelled 132, but we did not find a catalogue with this reference number.

## PATTERNS

**The number of** patterns in the collection is quite substantial; they form an important aspect of the whole. The presence of many original patterns and working designs allowed us to occasionally match them with completed items. The working designs are very simple, showing only a single solid inked line. The tape was tacked along this line, and the working of the grounds and fillings was left to the individual lacemaker's discretion. Many patterns are heavily pricked from numerous workings.

Occasionally a pattern was marked with stitch names, a number or details of its source, such as this:

**Pattern of Toilet Cover of Mrs Morgan sent to copy edging lace with net ground**
Size of cover without edging 48 ½" long by 9 ½" wide.
5 Squares let in about 2 ½ inches apart
Could be made with 3 or 4 squares.
Made up on linen lawn rather coarse.
No. 6 price 28/-

The patterns are drawn onto pink glazed linen, blind fabric, white architect's linen or butter paper (which is very fragile). Some patterns were made as rubbings of actual lace. Girvan's Irish Linen Stores often sent numbered rubbings of laces in their care to laceworkers for individual orders.

## THE LACE

✌ **Borris lace is** classified as a tape lace (braid guipure) in the category of mixed laces because it uses machine made tape with needlelace fillings. Tape lace is a more modern term for braid lace, point lace or point lacet.

The term guipure is also often applied, which indicates a lace having fixed parts connected by bars.[1] Some examples of Borris lace are strictly guipure, but in some instances the motifs are also connected by a net ground. Quite often, both bars and net ground connect the fixed parts. This description, from the *Powerhouse Museum Lace Collection: Glossary of Terms*, is useful:

> Tape laces, or 'mezzo punto' laces, were originally (17th C) laces made by tacking straight, separately made bobbin or hand-woven tapes around the outlines of a design and connecting them with decorative needle lace filling stitches and bars. In the nineteenth century this technique was revived and given various names, the most enduring of which is probably 'point lace'.[2]

In Borris lace, machine-made tape is laid in a continuous fashion over the design lines of the pattern which is drawn onto a firm fabric. The spaces within the design are decorated with filling stitches and these in turn are linked with net ground or picoted bars. Like most laces, Borris lace is time-consuming to produce, but the items are strong and durable and highly suited for use on clothing and household linen.

Borris lace seems to be the only substantive tape lace worked in Ireland. A few references have emerged relating to a novel tape lace made with tape and cord at Ardee, but this enterprise was short-lived.[3] 'Irish braid' and Irish lacet referred to the novelty braids like Cordon braid, which were used with crochet and advertised in *McCall's* magazines in the United States between 1903 and 1906, while an appliqué form of lacet on net was given the name Connemara lace in *Needlecraft Monthly Magazine* of February 2010.[4] These laces developed much later and may not even have originated in Ireland. They were known as domestic hobby laces, and required little skill and exertion.

Another Irish lace which used machine-made tape was Bandon lace, which involved tape appliquéd to organdie or cambric, producing another very different style categorised as embroidered lace.

The closest sister lace to Borris is the English Branscombe tape lace. The two laces appear comparable until you follow the pathway of the threads, when it becomes obvious that while they bear a strong resemblance the differences, summarised in the table on page 42, are most distinctive.

Familiarity with the classic stitches of needlelace puts one at risk of assuming that all similar techniques utilised these stitches. Marie's initial Borris lace project was

| COMPARISON OF BORRIS AND BRANSCOMBE LACES[5] | |
|---|---|
| **Borris lace characteristics** | **Branscombe lace characteristics** |
| Meandering designs with stylised shamrocks. Shamrocks are included in the designs of 23 items within the catalogue. | Flower designs are a feature, e.g. tulip. |
| Picots comprise 3 buttonhole stitches within the first stitch; 1–4 picots were used according to the length of the bar. | Picots are larger and more defined; called nibs, and comprise buttonholed loops. Single nibs were always worked in the centre of every bar. |
| Bars are straight and often parallel. Occasionally parallel pairs were worked in crag designs and occasionally short twisted bars were also used. | Bars are usually zigzagged and always have the distinctive nib in the centre. |
| Edging: knotted edge stitch (point de Venice) or single picot loops are most common. In Borris only 4 buttonhole stitches are worked into each loop. | Edging: Branscombe is always edged with a purl edge, which is a variation of the knotted edge stitch with 5 buttonhole stitches into each loop. |
| Spiders were rarely seen and not characteristic of Borris. A few woven spiders (uneven number of legs) have been catalogued. | Spiders were commonly used; ribbed spiders with an even number of legs (8) are characteristic. |
| Worked from the front. | Worked from the back. |
| Unique filling stitches. | Classic needlelace stitches are used for fillings. |
| Ground work used net ground or picoted bars. | Ground work always nibbed bars. |
| Tapes drawn up to neaten only as each section was worked. | All ruffled tape edges drawn up before embroidery was commenced. |
| Tapes rarely cross in designs, they just meet and separate to form areas of fills. A few exceptions are circular scrolls at the outside edge called a 'broken edge', the 'figure eight' edge (see Round crag d'oyley, Project 10) and the fir tree collar (Project 15). | Tapes regularly cross over each other to create flowing lines within the design. |
| Centres were mainly edged with knotted edge stitch. Sometimes two rows were worked with only 3 buttonhole stitches into each loop. | Spaced buttonhole stitch centres are called 'work arounds'. |

completed using the familiar classic stitches of Branscombe, but close comparison with photographs of the original pieces revealed obvious differences. We had at first identified pea stitch as a common filling, but quickly realised that it was in fact quite different from the Borris technique, which we call 'fine net with spaces' (having been unable to find the original name).

To our knowledge, no other lacemakers

have studied the original lace to ensure its genuine reproduction. After much trial and error, Marie is now confident that she is able to reproduce the stitches true to their original form. Marie's process was not unlike the early days of other lace adaptations. In 1865 Mrs Bury Palliser described how Mother Mary Ann Smith of the Presentation Convent in Youghal 'studied the lace that had come into her possession, examined the process by which it had been made, unravelled the threads one by one, and at last succeeded in mastering its many details'.[6]

Apart from knotted edge stitch (or point de Venice edging) and other needlelace edgings, most of the stitches and methods of working are unique to Borris lace and not to be found in the traditional literature and lace manuals. One exception was the serendipitous discovery of a stitch diagram in a Swedish book[7] which, although used for drawn thread work, was identical to the fine net stitch. The loose translation of the Swedish name seems to be 'antique' or 'heritage' stitch.

Most of the early tape laces employed either bars or net ground, but usually not both in the same piece. Borris lacemakers, however, happily combined bars and net ground in the one piece, as seen in the round d'oyley (catalogue no. 3).

Another similar technique is the *renda irlandesa* tape lace from Brazil which was introduced by Irish nuns; the Portuguese name translates as 'Irish point'. The modern form of this lace now bears a closer resemblance to Branscombe with the larger and more defined picots. Luxeuil lace from

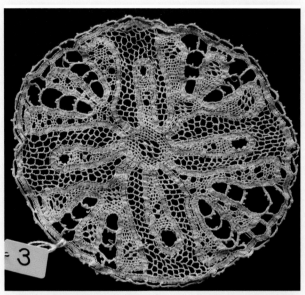

*This round d'oyley displays the use of both bars and net ground within the one piece (catalogue no. 3)*

France is less characteristic but in early times was called *guipure d'Irlande* after Irish needlelace.

## DESIGNS AND MOTIFS
### Lace with net ground

An eighteenth century Milanese flounce appears to have been the original inspiration and main influence for the creation of Borris lace with net ground. Part of the family lace, it comprises a very long flounce, 23 cm wide, which has been cut from a larger flounce, with what is probably an edging of later date along the cut edge.

The comparison of Stock Sample no. 36 with the Milanese flounce reveals similar design elements, although produced by the different techniques of bobbin lace and needle lace. The Borris net ground copies the round Milanese bobbin net ground, with commercial tape replacing the bobbin tape. In both examples, the design is a typical free-

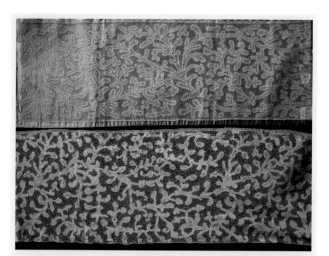

*Comparison of Stock Sample no. 36 with the flounce of Milanese style family lace*

*Stock Sampler 2. Most of the stock samples here reflect the Milanese style.*

flowing trail of stylised flowers with filling stitches worked into the small recesses of the tape. The machine-made tape is more difficult to manoeuvre and, as a result, in Borris lace the areas of filling stitches are larger. Both are edged with a similar and very decorative tape. Indeed most of the samples on Stock Sampler 2 reflect an attempt to closely imitate the Milanese style

### ✦ The crag design

A bobbin lace flounce and veil of family lace were most likely the catalyst for the crag design. These two items of bobbin lace (shown on p.36 and in detail opposite) have been identified by Rosemary Shepherd as Flemish (seventeenth and early eighteenth century) with no stylistic connections to Genoa, but some with Milan.

Family tradition believed them to be varieties of 'Coralline or Mermaid's Point where an unending tape winds through the piece and the design is merely held together by stout picoted bars'.[1] Coralline point was a Venetian needlelace, so named because the small meandering designs are said to have been inspired by the branching forms of coral. The Milanese and Flemish laces were in fact bobbin-made copies of the Venetian needlelaces. The Flemish characteristic of carrying continuous plaited bars across the back of solid areas and along the edge of motifs between bars in guipure lace is evident in the family lace examples.[2]

Crag was a local term for this guipure lace design. As with many of the facts about Borris lace, the origins of the name are lost in time,

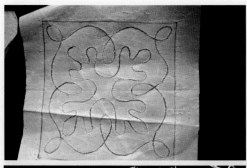

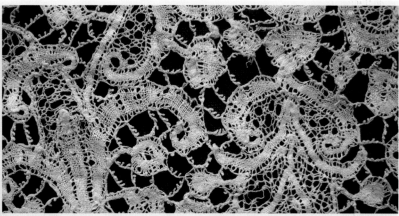

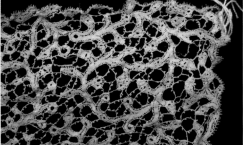

*Left: details of Flemish lace found in the family lace*
*Above: family lace showing continuous plaited threads from the bars carried*
*along the edges of the main lace, then plaited out to form the next bar*
*Below: crag design with original identifying label; account book showing*
*many entries for crag lace; pattern X coral lace (Mrs Douglas)*

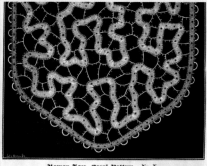

Roman Lace, Coral Pattern.—No. X.

but it could be a reference to the Blackstairs Mountains which form a scenic backdrop to the pretty town of Borris. Irish lacemakers would not have identified with coral, which is not found in their part of the world, so to name it 'crag', the familiar term for a rugged mountain, would have given it a local feel. Designs for this type of lace were common in the pattern books of the day and are often labelled 'coral,' as shown above.

The crag designs were strictly guipure, that is, they had no net ground. The bars are very short and the tape itself is the feature. The crag design is very distinctive; it was widely used, and popular, according to the evidence of the order books and delivered lace consignment lists.

The evidence seems to confirm that the specimens of old family lace in the collection were the early inspiration for the two distinct styles of Borris lace: Milanese style with net ground and decorative fillings, and crag. In a 1960 interview with Miss I.M. MacLeod, Mrs Alice Kavanagh revealed that when she visited Venice and Milan in 1932, she found 'the identical patterns were still being made and remarked that most of the Borris lace patterns had not varied from the pure Italian lace'.[3]

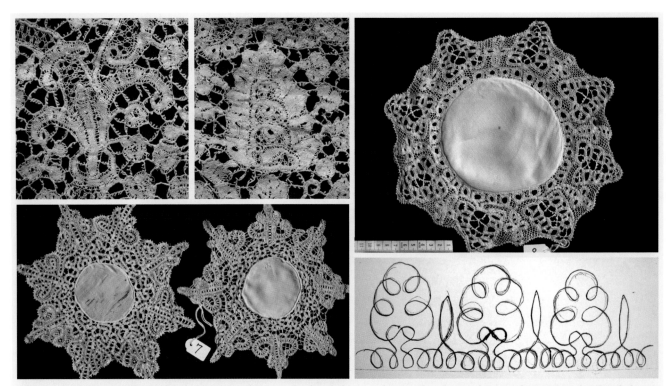

*Clockwise from top left: the fleur-de-lis motif seen in the family lace is often used in Borris designs; fir tree motif in family lace; fir tree motif in a centrepiece of Borris lace; original pattern for the fir tree design; items of Borris lace featuring the fleur-de-lis motif. These similar pieces show the work of two different lacemakers who have each applied their own interpretation of stitches*

### ⭢ Motifs copied from the family lace

The fleur-de-lis motif seen in the family lace is a common motif in the Borris designs. (See Project 6: Square trademark d'oyley.) The Borris fine net with spaces filling stitch also shows a close resemblance to the filling stitches of the old lace. The plaited picoted bars from the old lace are closely imitated by the guipure areas of the Borris designs, where the picoted bars are most often straight and parallel, sometimes crossing.

Another common motif in Borris lace is what we have called the 'fir tree'. Project 8, Fir tree handkerchief, and Project 15, Fir tree collar, are examples of how this motif was incorporated into designs.

### STITCH TECHNIQUES

⭢ **We are told** by Sarah Steele that Lady Kavanagh taught the lacemakers to copy her examples of old lace.[1] Because Borris lace was one of the early needlelaces of the revival period it is probable that they had little experience in needlelace techniques. (Youghal lace did not commence until six years later, in 1852.) The old lace was studied and copied in a unique way and 'under the direction of Lady Harriet, the women became skilled lacemakers'.[2]

The Borris lacemakers created some unique techniques which are not found in classic or modern lace manuals. When we commenced our cataloguing we had assumed that the classic stitches of needlelace would have been used, but detailed inspection revealed many surprises. We were disappointed to discover there was no local knowledge of the secrets of the stitches or their names. A few names are recorded on patterns and scribbled on stock sample cards, but other names can only be guessed at.

Marie rediscovered many secrets by carefully studying digital photographs of the lace and undoing some damaged fragments on loan to us. In place of the classic twisted buttonhole with wrapped return (point d'Espagne), we discovered what the Borris laceworkers called 'fine net' and 'net ground', which are variations of the usual classic stitches of needlelace. The twisted buttonhole stitch of Borris lace we have called a 'wrap' to distinguish the difference from the usual buttonhole stitch. In Borris lace it is always worked right to left, the opposite direction to the normal twisted buttonhole with wrapped return. A whip stitch over the bar completes each wrap stitch, locking the stitch into the characteristic neat square shape. What we thought we recognised as pea stitch was in fact a variation of the fine net with spaces. The picots also required detailed analysis to reproduce them in

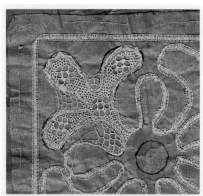

*Ballantrae lace, a work in progress belonging to Mrs Jean Dunlop of Ballantrae, showing the pathway of the threads; Marie's Eureka! The pathways of the fine net stitches are clearly seen*

a manner which reflected the original Borris pieces, and Marie has found that of all the picot techniques she has used this is by far the easiest and fastest to work – for the Borris lacemakers, time was money. The classic knotted edge stitch they used is also quicker to work then the purl edge used in Branscombe lace. The edging stitches and the buttonholed bars were the only familiar classic techniques.

Our understanding of the fine net stitch technique was confirmed when we saw Jean Leader's 2007 article on Ballantrae lace, showing a work in progress.[3] Being convinced that the techniques are identical, we were pleased to note the pathway of the thread showing it being taken across from left to right and on the return wrapping, then whipping after each stitch in turn, with the thread coming out under the base thread. In the classic needlelace stitches, the thread always comes out on top. The Borris technique produces foundation rows which are always perfectly straight and square with no distortion (this is similar to the ground in Burano lace).

When an area was completed, often the thread was not finished off but carried across the back of the tape to complete another section, as in the Flemish laces. Knots were sometimes used to start a new thread. Edgings for square cloths had to be gathered or mitred, as few patterns provided corner designs.

## DESIGN ELEMENTS

**Borris lace designs** are naïve, flowing and very stylised. Continuous lines of machine-made tape coil and meander to form pleasant shapes, the tape being folded or gathered into the design with very few sharp points. Older items in the collection often feature two parallel tapes joined to form narrow elongated shapes, or wide tapes running throughout an entire design with the tapes separating and rejoining at intervals. In most designs, the tapes do not cross, which is similar to bobbin tape lace but not usually characteristic of needle-made tape lace. The stylised three-leaf shamrock is a common feature and lends itself well to the free-flowing style. Other stylised elements include the pomegranate, fish, grapes, four-, five- and eight-petalled flowers, elongated fingers and leaves. The pomegranate, grapes and fish may have been used for church linen.

Designs were sometimes symmetrical, as seen in Project 16, Pomegranate and tree of life table centre. In symmetrical patterns the fillings used on the opposite sides usually match. All lace in the collection is either antique white or ecru in colour.

There are two distinct styles, often combined in the one design. The two styles are Milanese, described above, with a net ground, and crag, strictly a tape guipure with no mesh ground, in which a tightly meandering tape is

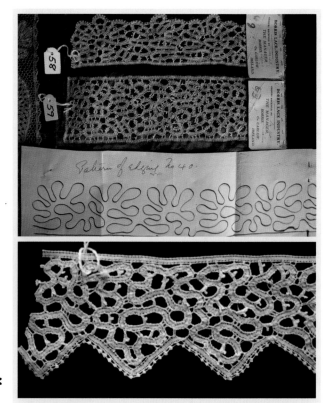

*Pattern with finished samples of crag pattern Vandyked edging 5 cm wide in the crag design (Catalogue item no. 13)*

held by short picoted bars that are sometimes in parallel pairs; occasionally twisted bars (without buttonhole stitches) are worked. At no point does the tape cross over itself. Crag has the appearance of Cornelli work. A piece of family lace was probably the inspiration. 'Crag' is used as a descriptive term on labels attached to stock samples; crag design was a popular order and appears in lists of lace received from the workers. Sixteen items are catalogued as crag design.

Bars in Borris lace are always decorated with picots, the number depending on the length of the bar, and the bars sometimes cross. More commonly they are regularly spaced, mostly parallel but occasionally curved. Picots often face the outside edge. Another feature which clearly differentiates Borris lace is the non-use of spider fillings, which are prolific in most other tape laces, probably because they are quickly worked.

The designs and techniques revealed in the collection changed and evolved over time, possibly reflecting the different tastes of the succession of Kavanagh ladies who oversaw the enterprise, changing fashions or perhaps the influence of the various work mistresses. The changes may also have resulted from the imaginations of the workers themselves, for the designs allowed a substantial amount of creativity in that the fillings could be interpreted by the lacemaker at whim.

## OUTLINE OF STITCHES
*See Stitch Glossary for detailed stitch diagrams.*

**Fine net stitch** is the most versatile and commonly used filling stitch. Fine net stitch with spaces was used to fill larger areas. This stitch is quite unique in the way that it is done.

**Woven blocks, woven block bars** and **parallel blocks** are also worked as filling stitches. Fine net stitches are packed together to form blocks. Most blocks are groups of 4 fine net stitches packed closely together. These blocks are found within fine net fillings and can be single, or grouped, that is, as four-block or nine-block variations. Sometimes they were worked to fill the whole length, as in parallel blocks. They were also spaced in step fashion in circular or curved areas. These blocks, or the patterns of holes they produce, are similar to the ornamental holes or windows in the linen stitch of the bobbin-made tapes of Milanese style lace.

**Net ground (double wrap stitch)** is not the usual twisted buttonhole with wrapped return (point d'Espagne). Net ground is commonly found in pieces within the collection and rows can face in any direction, but usually along the longest run or whatever was convenient.

**Picoted bars, parallel pairs** or **spaced parallel bars** connect larger spaces. Picots on picoted bars usually face towards the outside edge and the number is dependent on the length of the bar.

**Borris picots** involve the working of 3 buttonhole stitches into the forward loop of a spaced buttonhole stitch. The next buttonhole stitch should be pulled firmly up against the picot to avoid leaving a loop; we have seen many loops on the edges of picots in the collection which have led others to believe that the picots were worked on a pin, as in Venetian picots.

**Knotted edge stitch,** also known as **point de Venice**. Some very small circular areas are also edged with a row of knotted edge stitch using only 3 buttonhole stitches (instead of 4) into each loop.

**Single loop with picot edge** is the most common edging found. Other edgings include pyramid loop with picot, and knotted edge stitch.

**Double elongated net ground** is yet another new stitch, only evident in catalogued items 10 and 17. This stitch is worked in narrow elongated spaces.

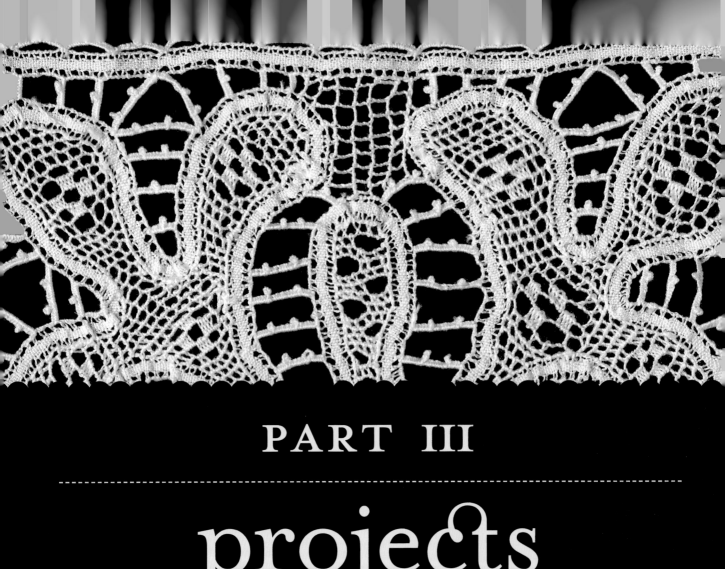

# PART III

## projects

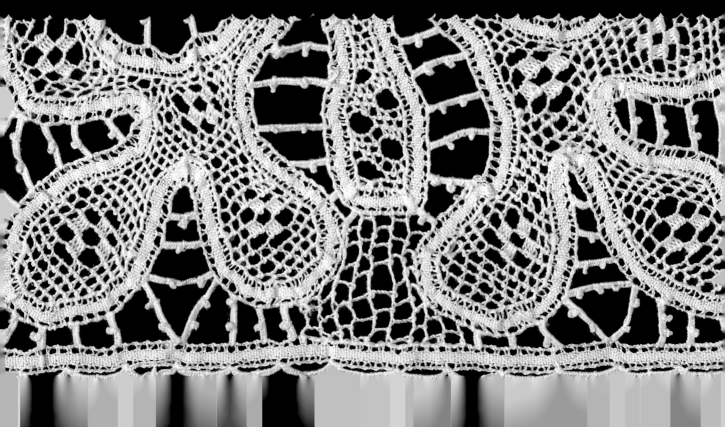

*All sixteen project designs presented in this section have been copied or adapted from patterns found in the Borris Lace Collection and worked by Marie Laurie. With these projects you also have a valuable resource of finishing techniques.*

Marie has shown many different finishing techniques for attaching lace to linen. As a show judge for many years, Marie has seen many excellent pieces of lace ruined by careless or unskilled finishing. Choose from among the variations or work each one to build up your skills and knowledge.

All projects use the following needles: sharps no. 10 for tacking and ballpoint no. 26 for working the lace. All projects have been worked with Madeira Cotona no. 30, but DMC no. 30 or an equivalent 100% cotton thread are also suitable. Small sharp embroidery scissors are essential, as is a thimble for those who use one.

We strongly suggest that Project 1 is worked first to gain a clear understanding of the unique techniques employed by the workers of Borris lace. Once these basic skills are acquired, you will be able to move onto the more advanced projects and start to create your own variations.

The instructions for each project include a photograph of the finished piece, the project design, the requirements, and additional tips and techniques. Refer to the photographs of the projects for the placement of stitches.

Borris lacemakers always adapted designs from elsewhere. If you keep to the design principles and the classic stitches detailed within this book you can call your lace 'in the style of Borris lace'.

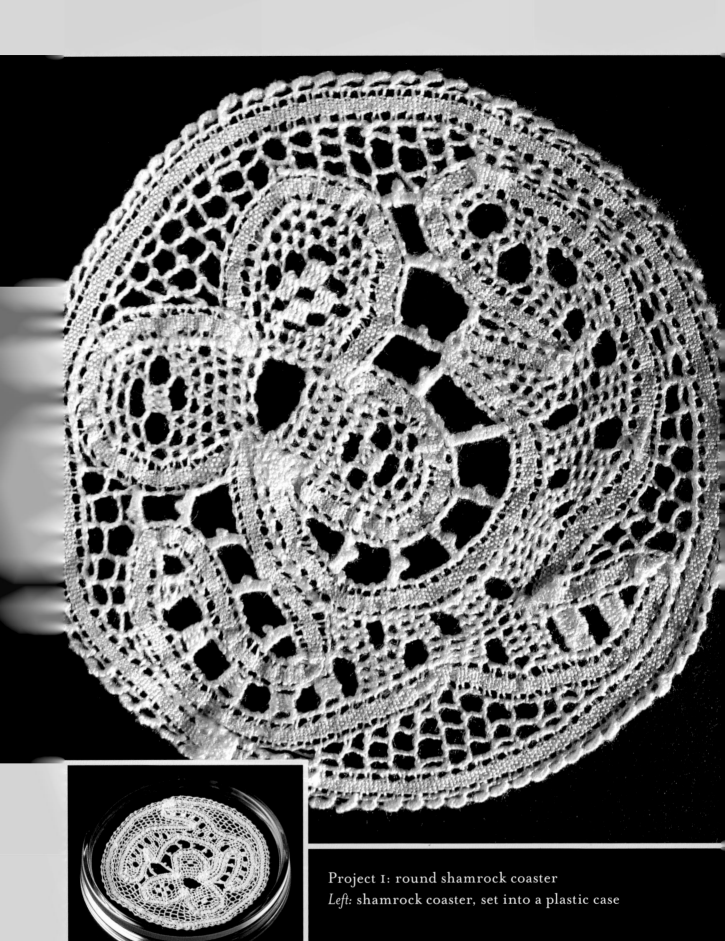

Project 1: round shamrock coaster
*Left*: shamrock coaster, set into a plastic case

# round shamrock coaster

------------------------------------ ❋ ------------------------------------

*This is a beginner sampler using all the basic Borris techniques.*
*Finished size: 7.5 cm (3 inches) diameter.*

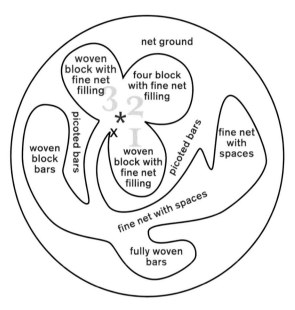

## PATTERN & STITCH GUIDE
★ circular recess edged in knotted edge stitch

## REQUIREMENTS

❋ calico or strong cotton fabric 18 cm square

❋ pattern traced onto blue tissue paper

❋ clear Contact adhesive
(slightly larger than the pattern)

❋ needles: sharps no. 10 for tacking and
ballpoint no. 26 for working the lace

❋ thread: Madeira Cotona no. 30, DMC no. 30
or equivalent 100% cotton thread

❋ small sharp embroidery scissors

❋ thimble if used

❋ 1 m (40 in) narrow tape: No. 6 tape (the
narrowest) is a plain straight tape with no
gathering threads to be drawn up

## PREPARING THE ASSEMBLY

Centre pattern tracing on top of a piece of calico or
strong cotton which is slightly larger than the design.
Cover with a piece of Contact, larger than the design
so that it connects the pattern to the calico while also
strengthening and protecting the pattern. Tack all
layers together around the outside edge of the design
using a sharp needle and tacking thread.

This process is always referred to as 'the assembly'.

*The prepared assembly*

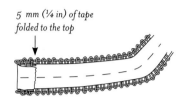

*Diagram 1: Laying the tape*

5 mm (¼ in) of tape
folded to the top

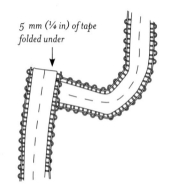

5 mm (¼ in) of tape
folded under

*Diagram 2: Enclosing the end of the tape*

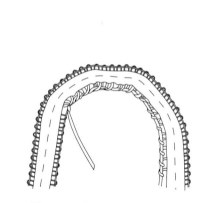

*Diagram 3: Drawing up the tape*

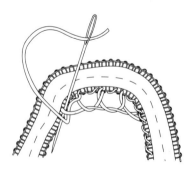

*Diagram 4: Fine net filling, row 1*

## LAYING THE TAPE

The lines of the design show the placement of the tape only. Thread the sharps needle with a normal length of tacking thread with a knot in the end. With the knot at the back of the fabric, commence tacking the tape to the assembly, making sure to centre it on the design lines. There is no right or wrong side to the tape. Commence at X by folding over 5 mm (¼ in) of the end of the tape to the top. See diagram 1.

Stitches should be small and firm. Ensure that the outer curve of the tape lies flat. This will mean that the inner curve is ruffled. This ruffling will be dealt with when the decorative filling stitches are worked. Keeping the continuous line of the tape, fold the tape at the sharp points of the shamrock and any other sharp turnings. Continue around design until tapes meet at the starting point. Finish by turning under 5 mm (1/4 in) of tape and place on top of starting fold, thus enclosing all raw edges. This is very important for a neat finish. See diagram 2. Finish off the tacking thread on the back of the assembly. Tack tape around the edge of the design in the same manner.

## METHOD

### SHAMROCK LEAFLET ONE

Using the ballpoint needle, begin at starting point X at the base of leaflet 1. Oversew the inner edge of the tape up the right-hand side of the leaflet (incorporating the tail end of the thread as you work) and across the top to the row 1 starting point. See diagram 3. The remaining edge of the tape will be oversewn as you work the filling.

The following decorative filling stitches are used: net ground, fine net with spaces, woven block, four block, woven block bar, circular recess edged in knotted edge stitch, fully woven block bars and picoted bars.

### Fine net filling

**Row 1:** Starting at the top left-hand side of the leaflet (see diagram 4), take the thread across to the opposite side by stitching into the edge of the tape opposite.

Pick up the edge of the tape at a point above the first stitch, and bring the thread out on the right-hand side, giving a single wrap. Now whip the base thread once to complete the stitch sequence. NB: Wrap the vertical, then whip the base thread, to complete each fine net filling stitch. Work another 2 stitches to complete the row. Oversew down the left hand side of the tape to position for the next row.

**TIP** Pull down firmly after whipping the base thread to lock each stitch and ensure an even tension.

**Row 2:** Again, take the base thread across to the opposite side and fill row by working 1 stitch into each space between the stitches of the previous row above. Increase as the shape widens by adding stitches at the beginning or end of a row (diagram 5).

**TIP** Direction lines for rows of fillings can be scored onto the design if preferred.

These two rows form the basic fine net filling stitch which is one of the main components of Borris lace. As you progress you will learn many variations of this basic technique.

### Woven block with fine net filling

**Row 1:** Take thread across, work 2 stitches, leave an open space by missing 1 space above (whipping the base thread twice), then work 2 more stitches to complete the row (diagram 6).

**Row 2:** Take thread across and work 1 stitch, then leave an open space by missing 1 space above and whipping the base twice. Work a single woven block of 4 closely worked fine net stitches into the space on the base thread above. Leave an open space, whip base thread twice, then work 1 more fine net stitch to complete the row (diagram 7).

**Row 3:** Take thread across, work 1 fine net stitch at edge, then 2 stitches into the empty space above. Leave a space below the woven block (remembering to whip the base thread twice), followed by 2 fine net stitches into space above and finally 1 fine net stitch at edge to complete the row (diagram 8).

**Row 4:** Take thread across, work back, remembering to work 2 stitches into the space above (diagram 9).

Continue rows of plain fine net filling to fill the remaining area.

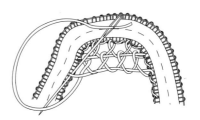

*Diagram 5: Fine net filling, row 2*

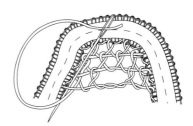

*Diagram 6: Woven block, row 1*

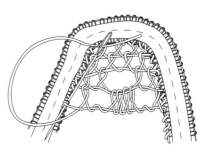

*Diagram 7: Woven block, row 2*

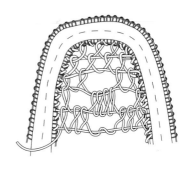

*Diagram 8: Woven block, row 3*

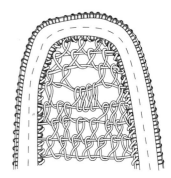

*Diagram 9: Woven block, row 4*

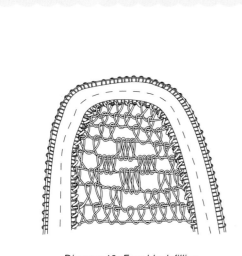

*Diagram 10: Four-block filling*

## SHAMROCK LEAFLET TWO

### Four-block filling

Begin leaflet 2 in the same manner as previous leaflet but work 5 stitches instead of 3 to give extra room for the placement of the blocks. This leaflet is larger and will easily accommodate the extra stitches. Study diagram 10 and you will see that it is only an extension of the previously detailed instructions for leaflet 1.

To finish off a thread, whip forward along the edge of the tape for about 1 cm and cut off neatly. Rethread the needle and commence by incorporating the tail of your new thread as you work up or down the edge of the tape (also incorporating the previous tail).

## SHAMROCK LEAFLET THREE

The third leaflet is worked in the same manner as leaflet 1.

### Woven block bars

Woven block bars are worked to fill small elongated areas between tapes. Commence by oversewing the inner edge of the tape on the right of the space to reduce the gathers and neaten to the point where you wish to begin the first block. See diagram 11.

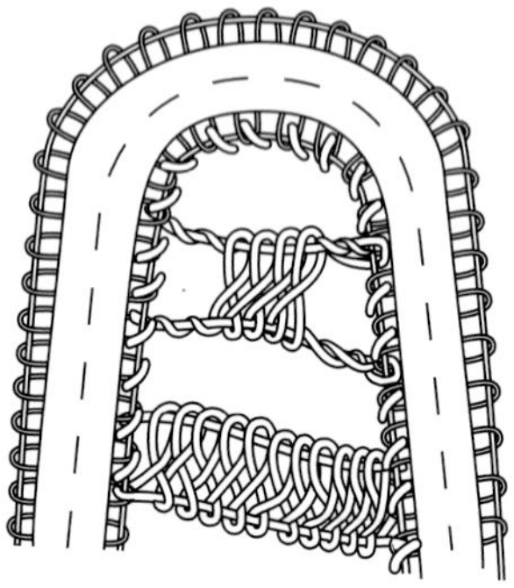

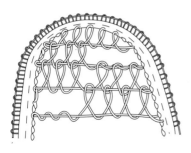

*Diagram 11: Woven block bar*

From the left side of the space, take thread across, whip back. The number of whips depends upon the size of the space to be filled. In this instance use 4 whips.

Oversew down to the next row level. Take thread across. Whip back to the starting point of the block. Work a block of 4 fine net filling stitches close together. Whip the remaining space on the base thread to complete the row.

Continue working blocks to fill the space.

For variation, whole bars can be filled with fine net filling stitches to produce a fully woven block bar like the second bar in diagram 11.

### Fine net with spaces

We have been unable to find any reference to this stitch technique in the collection at Borris, so we have given it the descriptive title of fine net

*Diagram 12: Fine net with spaces*

with spaces. It is mainly used to fill larger areas. See diagram 12.

Commence by drawing up the right hand edge of the tape if required.
**Row 1:** Starting at the top left hand side of the area to be filled, work 1 row of evenly spaced, fine net filling.

**Row 2:** As you work back over the base thread, leave a hole by missing 3 spaces in the row above, remembering to whip the base thread 3 times, then complete the row with the required number of stitches. Oversew down the left hand side of the tape to position for the next row.

**Row 3:** Work another row of fine net filling stitches but take care to work 3 fine net stitches into the space made by the previous row.

Continue this sequence, positioning spaces on alternate sides in the alternate rows. Ensure that the spaces on the base thread are covered with the appropriate number of whips. In a wider area, open spaces can also be positioned in the centre of rows, or twice in the one row.

### Net ground
Study of the work in the collection has shown that this stitch (diagram 13) was mainly worked as a background filling. It was worked in any direction, often changing direction as necessary. It is important however to be consistent with spacing and tension to achieve a neat square stitch.

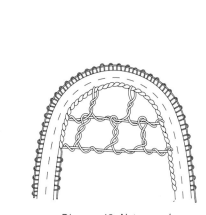

*Diagram 13: Net ground*

**TIP** Work in short rows where you can easily stitch into the side of a tape or the purl edge of a buttonhole bar.

Commence in the same manner as for fine net filling but work double-wrap stitches (add a second wrap or twist) with 2 whips between each double-wrap stitch on the base thread. The extra wrap results in a larger stitch.

**TIP** Pull each whip stitch firmly to lock the stitch into position.

### Picoted bar
This picot required much research and study. Depending on the size of the bar to be worked, 1, 2 or 3 picots can be included. The picots usually face out towards the edge of the work.

If necessary, draw up the left hand edge of the tape to neaten. Start at

**TIP** Anchor the picot with your fingernail while pulling up the next buttonhole stitch on the bar to stop it being caught up.

**TIP** If you find that you cannot start on the right hand side, it is permissible to lay an extra (fourth) foundation thread across the bar to position yourself for working buttonhole stitch.

the top of the right hand side at the point where the first bar is needed. Lay 3 foundation threads between the tape edges and work back, covering the foundation threads with neat, firm buttonhole stitches until you reach the centre of the bar where a picot is required. Work a loose buttonhole stitch, then work 3 buttonhole stitches into the forward loop of this buttonhole stitch. Continue working buttonhole stitches to complete the bar, taking care to pull the first one firmly to the left to close up the space where the picot was worked. This produces a very fast and neat picot.

It is most important to complete the bar by bringing the needle up from underneath through the tape edge. This will ensure that the bar sits flat. Oversew down the edge of the tape to the position of the next picoted bar. See diagram 14.

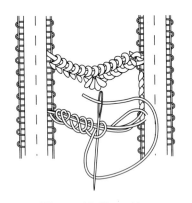

*Diagram 14: Picoted bar*

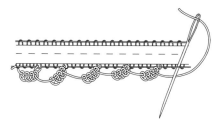

*Diagram 15: Knotted edge stitch or point de Venice edging*

## EDGINGS
----------

Items in the collection display a variety of needlelace edgings; others are finished with machine-made tapes of various styles.

### Knotted edge stitch or point de Venice edging

Many items were worked with a point de Venice variation, which is similar to the shell stitch of Youghal needlepoint lace. See diagram 15.

Attach the thread to the outer edge of the tape with a buttonhole stitch and work over the tail. Working from left to right, work a spaced buttonhole stitch. Holding the thread to the left, there are now 2 threads over which you work 4 neat buttonhole stitches. Repeat this stitch into every 3 or 4 holes along the edge of the tape.

This stitch is also used to edge inner circles within designs after neatening the tape. Work one row incorporating only 3 buttonhole stitches into each loop to fill the centre of the shamrock.

## FINISHING
-------------

On completing the lace, snip the tacking from the back of the assembly. Remove the lace and use tweezers to pull out any remaining pieces of tacking thread. Wash the lace if necessary and press gently under an ironing cloth.

# quare shamrock pincushion

❋

*ushion finished size: 8.5 cm (3 ½ in) square. Lace finished size: 8 cm (3 ¼ in) square*

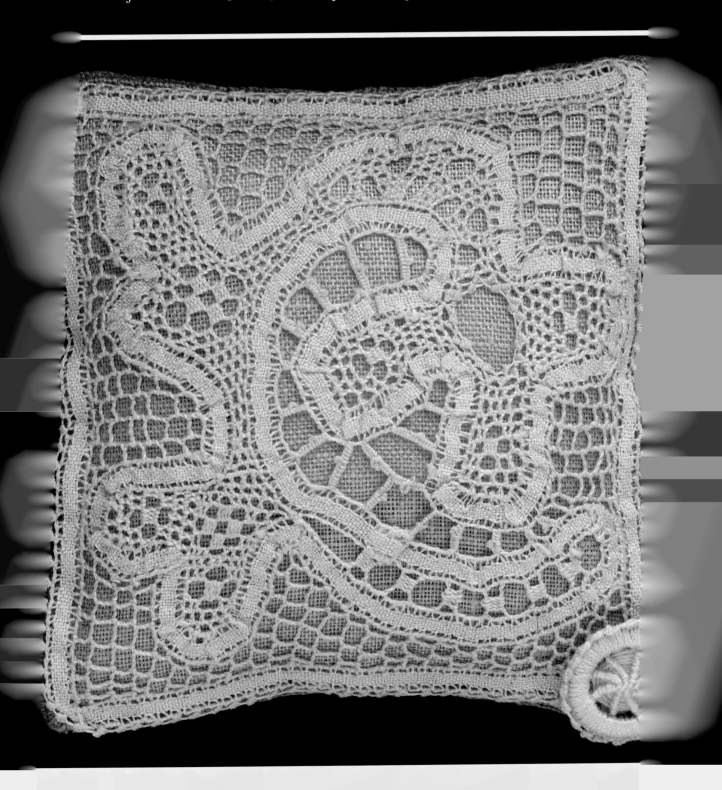

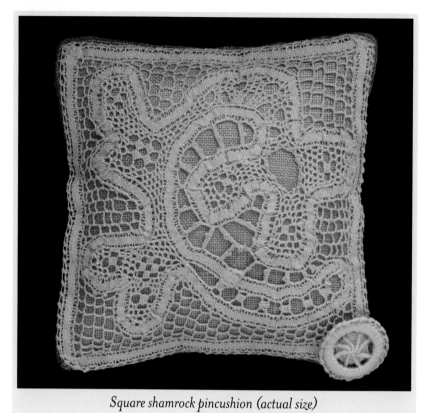

*Square shamrock pincushion (actual size)*

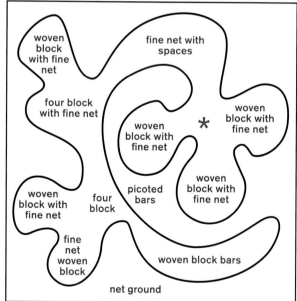

woven block with fine net

fine net with spaces

four block with fine net

woven block with fine net

woven block with fine net

woven block with fine net

woven block with fine net

picoted bars

four block

woven block with fine net

fine net woven block

woven block bars

net ground

## PATTERN & STITCH GUIDE
★ circular recess edged in knotted edge stitch

## REQUIREMENTS

- calico or strong cotton fabric 18 cm square
- pattern traced onto blue tissue paper
- clear Contact adhesive (slightly larger than the pattern)
- needles: sharps no. 10 for tacking and ballpoint no. 26 for working the lace
- thread: Madeira Cotona no. 30, DMC no. 30 or equivalent 100% cotton thread
- small sharp embroidery scissors
- thimble if used
- 1 m (40 in) narrow tape: No. 6 tape (the narrowest) is a plain straight tape with no gathering threads to be drawn up
- fabric approx. 25 x 12 cm (10 in x 5 in)
- sewing cotton to match
- 1.5 cm (⅝ in) flat round washer with 7.5 mm (⅜ in) central hole (or a pretty button with shank)

## METHOD

Prepare an assembly 18 cm (7 in) square and lay the tape in a continuous placement of the design.

### FILLING

Work the design as detailed for the round shamrock coaster, using the same decorative filling stitches.

The centre of the shamrock leaf is edged with 1 row of knotted edge stitch, incorporating only 3 buttonhole stitches into each loop.

### EDGING

The edge is finished with knotted edge stitch as described for the shamrock coaster.

### FINISHING

Snip the tacking stitches from the back of the assembly and remove the lace. Pre-shrink both lace and linen, and press gently under an ironing cloth. Cut the linen in half to produce two 12 cm (5 in) square pieces.

Starting 1.5 cm ($^5/_8$ in) in from the edge, withdraw a thread on each side of both pieces of linen to mark out squares slightly larger than the lace. Work chain stitch over the space of the withdrawn threads using matching thread. Cover the chain stitch with a row of neat buttonhole stitches. To join the pieces together, work another row of buttonhole stitches, picking up the two purl edges of the buttonholed rows of the two linen squares. Leave a small opening. Stuff firmly, ensuring that the corners are well filled. Close the opening by completing the buttonholed row.

Centre the lace on top of the filled pincushion and attach by slip stitching along the inside edge of the outer row of tape.

The decorative 'button' has been covered in the Dorset technique. Cover the washer with buttonhole stitches, then work a row of knotted edge stitch. Into the centre work your favourite spider filling. Attach the 'button' to one corner of the pincushion. It can be used as a hanger for a pair of embroidery scissors to which you have attached a small loop of ribbon.

**TIP** It is neater to begin the tape attachment at a point away from the corner. Remember to begin with folded tape uppermost and finish with tape end folded under, leaving no raw edges.

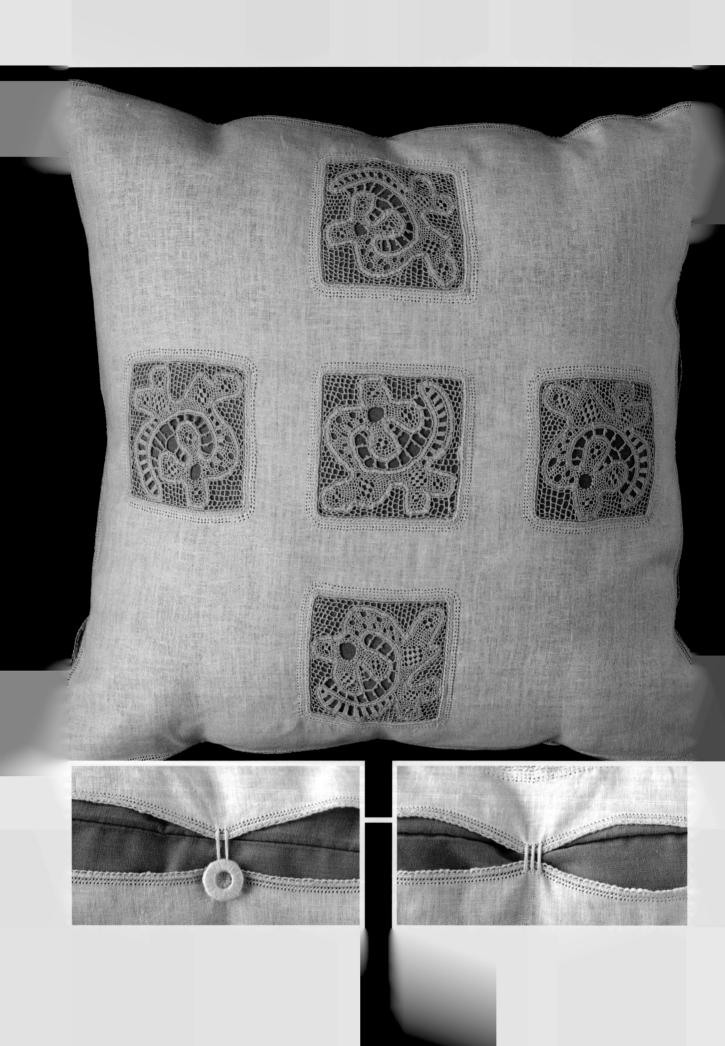

# cushion with square shamrock insertions

---------------------------------❋---------------------------------

*These inserts were often applied in chequerboard patterns.*
*Finished size of cushion: 38 cm (15 in) square. Lace insertions: 8 cm (3 ⅛ in) square*

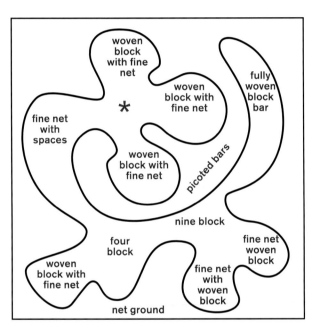

## PATTERN & STITCH GUIDE

★ circular recess edged in knotted edge stitch
*note the pattern has been reversed for some inserts*

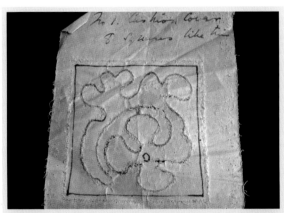

*A well-used pattern for the shamrock cushion cover insert; from the Borris House collection*

## REQUIREMENTS

* calico or strong cotton fabric 18 cm (7 in) square
* pattern traced onto blue tissue paper
* clear Contact adhesive (slightly larger than the pattern)
* needles: sharps no. 10 for tacking and ballpoint no. 26 for working the lace
* thread: Madeira Cotona no. 30, DMC no. 30 or equivalent 100% cotton thread
* small sharp embroidery scissors
* thimble if used
* 5 m (5 ¼ yds) narrow tape
* handkerchief linen or fine cotton approx. 45 x 90 cm (18 x 35 ½ in)
* heavy brown paper
* 3 medium sized buttons
* cushion insert 43 cm (17 in) square
* cover cushion insert with linen cover 38 cm (15 in) square, in your choice of colour

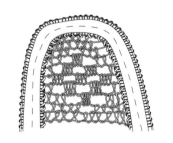

*Diagram 16: Nine-block woven filling*

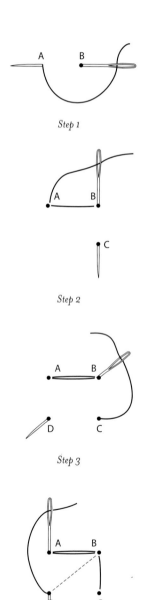

*Step 1*

*Step 2*

*Step 3*

*Step 4*

*Diagram 17: Four-sided stitch*

## METHOD

Prepare an assembly 18 cm (7 in) square and lay the tape in a continuous placement of the design.

Work five repeats of the shamrock square as detailed for the pincushion in Project 2. For variation, work a nine-block filling (diagram 16) where space allows. Omit the knotted edge stitch on all squares.

### Nine-block filling

This stitch is suitable for larger areas. Start with at least two rows of fine net filling. If you are filling the centre of a leaf, commence in the same manner as for four-block filling (see diagram 10), with 5 fine net stitches. Add the extension of 3 woven blocks at the centre point before completing the diamond layout of nine blocks. Complete the filling using 2 or more rows of fine net filling.

## FINISHING

Snip the tacking stitches from the back of the assembly and remove the lace. Pre-shrink both lace and linen, and press gently under an ironing cloth. Cut the linen in half to produce two 45 cm square pieces.

Pin the lace squares in place onto one square of the linen, and attach with a tacking stitch. Finally attach the lace to the linen by working a row of buttonhole stitch around each square of lace, with the purl edge of the buttonhole stitch towards the lace. On the purl edge of the buttonhole stitch work knotted edge stitch (see diagram 15).

Cut away the fabric from behind the lace, leaving an allowance of 1 cm (1/2 in) all around. Fold this excess fabric back on itself and tack in place. Work a row of four-sided stitch (diagram 17 and directions below), through both layers of linen. Trim off the remainder of fabric before working a second row of four-sided stitch to neaten the back and make the join strong. Repeat this process for each insertion.

### Four-sided stitch

**Step 1:** Working vertically down the row, bring needle up at A, down at B.

**Step 2:** Bring needle up again at A and down at B, then bring needle up four threads down below B at C

**Step 3:** Bring needle down at B, and up diagonally across to D.

**Step 4:** Bring needle down at A and up at D again to complete the stitch.

D now becomes A for the second four-sided stitch. Repeat down each side of the insertion. Check for one diagonal thread behind each worked stitch on the reverse side of the embroidery.

### Four-sided stitch with knotted edge stitch

This edging combination was shown to me by a Hungarian embroiderer many years ago. I always use this method to work a straight edge even if a thread is not removed. It gives a very strong edge (diagram 18).

**Step 1:** Approximately 3 cm in from the edges of the linen, withdraw one thread, leave 4, withdraw another thread, and over the 4 threads work 1 row of four-sided stitch (see diagram 17).

**Step 2:** From the outer side of the four-sided stitch, leave 5 threads, remove 2, and over the 5 threads work chain stitch.

**Step 3:** Working left to right, work 4 buttonhole stitches into each hole of the four-sided stitch. These buttonhole stitches cover the chain stitch and should fit into the space of the withdrawn thread. Trim fabric close to the purl edge of the buttonhole stitch.

**Step 4:** To complete, tack the work to a double layer of brown paper (which gives you something to hang onto to make it easier to work and control your tension), and work a row of knotted edge stitch.

Repeat this edging for the second side of the cushion.

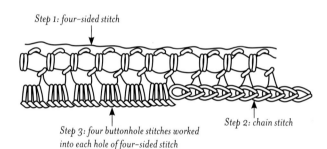

*Step 1: four-sided stitch*

*Step 2: chain stitch*

*Step 3: four buttonhole stitches worked into each hole of four-sided stitch*

*Diagram 18: Steps 1–3 for edging of four-sided stitch, chain stitch and buttonhole stitch (Step 4, knotted edge stitch, not shown)*

### ASSEMBLY

Join the cushion cover pieces with 3 sets of buttonholed bars on each of three sides (see detail photo). Close the fourth side by attaching three buttons and working buttonhole loops to match (see detail photo).

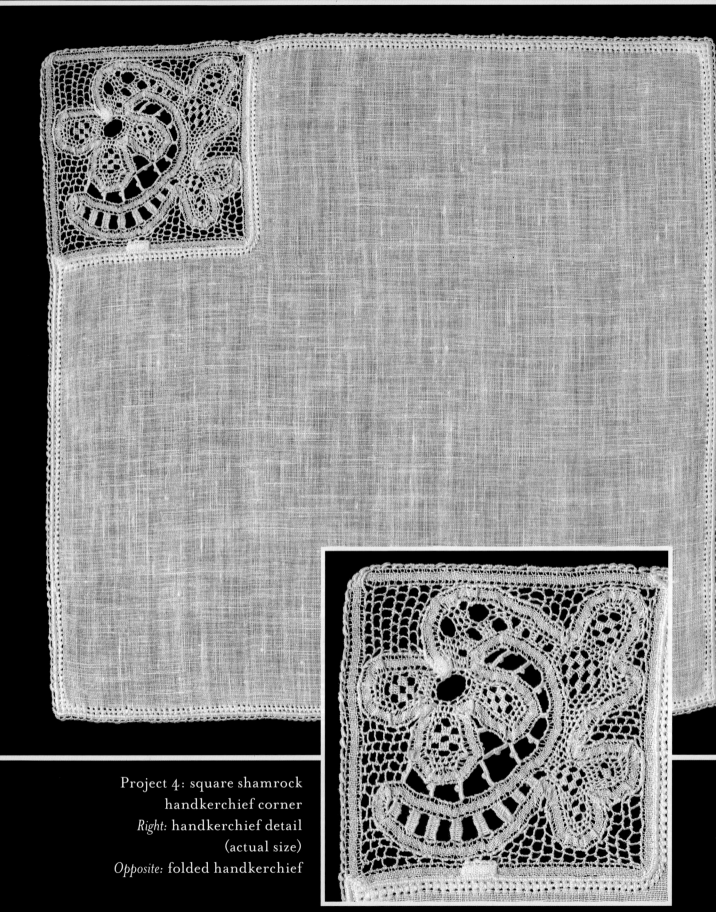

Project 4: square shamrock
handkerchief corner
*Right:* handkerchief detail
(actual size)
*Opposite:* folded handkerchief

# square shamrock handkerchief corner

------------------------------- ❋ -------------------------------

*Finished size of handkerchief: 25 cm (10 in) square. Lace insertion: 8 cm (3 ⅛ in) square*

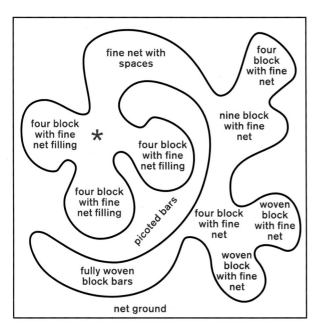

## PATTERN & STITCH GUIDE
★ circular recess edged in knotted edge stitch

### REQUIREMENTS

* calico or strong cotton fabric 18 cm (7 in) square
* pattern traced onto blue tissue paper
* clear Contact adhesive (slightly larger than the pattern)
* needles: sharps no. 10 for tacking and ballpoint no. 26 for working the lace
* thread: Madeira Cotona no. 30, DMC no. 30 or equivalent 100% cotton thread
* small sharp embroidery scissors
* thimble if used
* 1 m (40 in) narrow tape
* handkerchief linen or fine cotton approx. 30 cm (12 in) square
* heavy brown paper

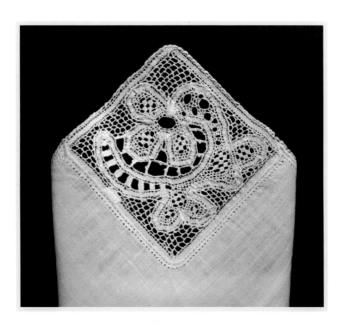

# ❋ square shamrock handkerchief corner

**METHOD**

Prepare an assembly 18 cm (7 in) square and lay the tape in a continuous placement of the design.

Work as detailed for the shamrock coaster in project 1, or to your own preference, but do not work the knotted edge stitch edging. For variation, work a nine-block filling where space allows (see diagram 16, Project 3).

**FINISHING**

Snip the tacking stitches from the back of the assembly and remove the lace. Pre-shrink the linen and lace, and press both pieces.

Pin the lace square onto one corner of the linen and attach with tacking stitches. Work a row of buttonhole stitches (stitch into both lace and linen) around these two insertion edges with the purl edge of the buttonhole stitch towards the lace. Withdraw a thread from the linen in line with the outer edges of the tape along two outer edges of the handkerchief. Withdraw threads on the other two sides to match. Work chain stitch over the space of the withdrawn threads. Cover the chain stitch with fine buttonhole stitch. Carefully cut away excess fabric from the buttonhole edges and behind the lace.

Tack the handkerchief to strong brown paper and work a row of knotted edge stitch around all four sides of the handkerchief. A row of four-sided stitch (diagram 17) should be worked up against the row of buttonhole stitch

# PROJECT 5
# bookmark

❋

*Learn a new stitch: double elongated net stitch; and a new edging: single loop with picot.*
*Finished size: 19.5 x 6 cm (7 ⅝ x 2 ⅜ in)*

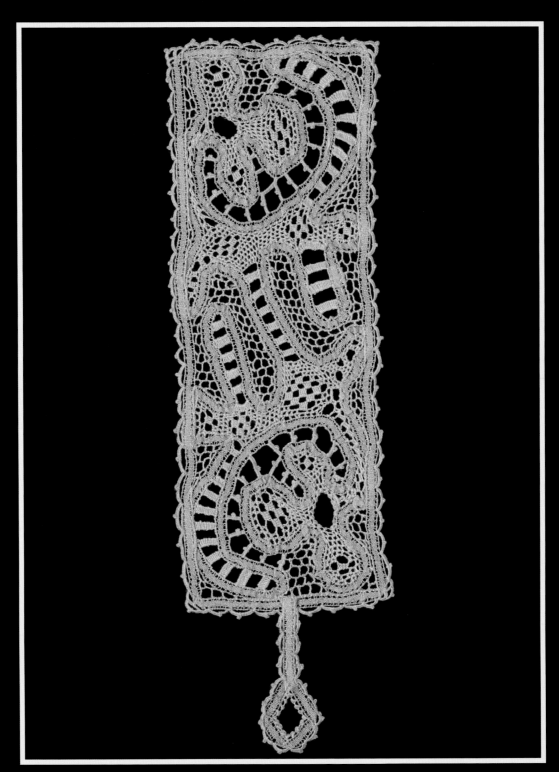

# ❋ bookmark

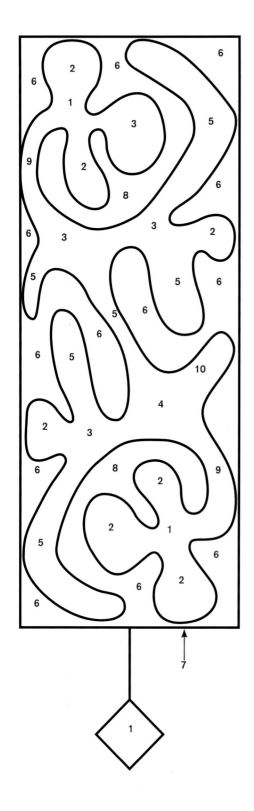

## REQUIREMENTS

- calico or strong cotton fabric 26 x 16 cm (10 ¼ x 6 ¼ in)
- pattern traced onto blue tissue paper
- clear Contact adhesive (slightly larger than the pattern)
- needles: sharps no. 10 for tacking and ballpoint no. 26 for working the lace
- thread: Madeira Cotona no. 30, DMC no. 30 or equivalent 100% cotton thread
- small sharp embroidery scissors
- thimble if used
- 2 m (2 yds 7 in) narrow tape

### PATTERN & STITCH GUIDE

1  recesses edged in knotted edge stitch
2  woven block with fine net filling
3  four-block with fine net filling
4  nine-block with fine net filling
5  fully woven block bars
6  net ground
7  single loop with picot edging all around bookmark
8  picoted bars
9  double elongated net stitch
10  fine net with spaces

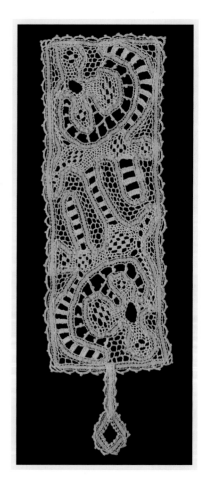

## METHOD

Prepare an assembly 26 x 16 cm (10 ¼ x 6 ¼ in) and lay the tape in a continuous placement of the design.

Finish the inner edge of the diamond-shaped space in the tag with knotted edge stitch as for circular recesses.

### Double elongated net stitch

Commence this stitch in the same way as net ground (see diagram 13, Project 1), that is, work 1 whip on the base thread, 2 double-wrap stitches, together, then a final whip. There is no whip between the double-wrap stitches, so the two stitches remain close together. Always work both stitches to the left of the previous stitch for a left hand curve, reverse for a right hand curve.

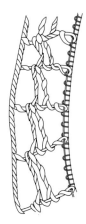

*Diagram 19: Double elongated net stitch*

## EDGING

The bookmark is finished with a single loop with picot edge. Many of the original lace samples in the collection had this finish to the tape. The semi-circular bars are spaced about 5 or 6 holes apart along the tape (diagram 20).

### Single loop with picot

Lay two foundation loops of threads, working from left to right then right to left. Working left to right, cover the loop with 10 buttonhole stitches, then work a picot as detailed in diagram 14, Project 1. Complete the loop with another 10 buttonhole stitches.

**TIP** Loops should overlap just slightly for a neater and more regular appearance. To do this, place needle into the previous hole in the edge of the tape just to the left of the last loop, as seen in diagram 20.

*Diagram 20: Single loop with picot*

**TIP** Starting a new thread on a loop edging. Leave a long tail on the right hand side of first loop placement. Take thread across to the left, back, then across again to give a three-thread foundation to the first loop. After covering the loop with 10 buttonhole stitches the tail can be cut off close to the work. All loop stitches and picoted bars can be commenced in this way.

## FINISHING

Snip the tacking stitches from the back of the assembly and gently press the lace under an ironing cloth.

# square trademark d'oyley

※

*This project is adapted from a pattern in the collection, Catalogue item no. 1, pattern no. 1, which was a trademark design of the Borris Lace Industry. Finished size: 15 cm (6 in) square*

**PATTERN**  enlarge pattern by 180%

## REQUIREMENTS

- calico or strong cotton fabric 22 cm (8 ½ in) square
- pattern traced onto blue tissue paper
- clear Contact adhesive (slightly larger than the pattern)
- needles: sharps no. 10 for tacking and ballpoint no. 26 for working the lace
- thread: Madeira Cotona no. 30, DMC no. 30 or equivalent 100% cotton thread
- small sharp embroidery scissors
- thimble if used
- 3.5 m (3 ¾ yds) narrow tape

*Catalogue item no. 1, pattern no. 1*

# ❋ square trademark d'oyley

**METHOD**

Prepare an assembly 22 cm (8 ½ in) square, and lay the tape in a continuous placement of the design

This d'oyley was worked with many variations of filling stitches. Choose your favourites from the stitch glossary or use the photographs of the finished d'oyleys as your guide for placement.

**EDGING**

The outside edge of the tape is finished with a single loop with picot edging (see diagram 20).

**FINISHING**

Snip the tacking stitches from the back of the assembly and gently press the lace under an ironing cloth.

*Catalogue item no. 2; this original has no edging and may*
*have been intended as an insertion*

# PROJECT 7
# round floral d'oyley

---------------------------- ※ ----------------------------

*This design is adapted from Catalogue item no. 4. Five similar pieces were found in the collection.*
*All reflected the makers' own choices of fillings. Finished size: 15 cm (6 in) diameter*

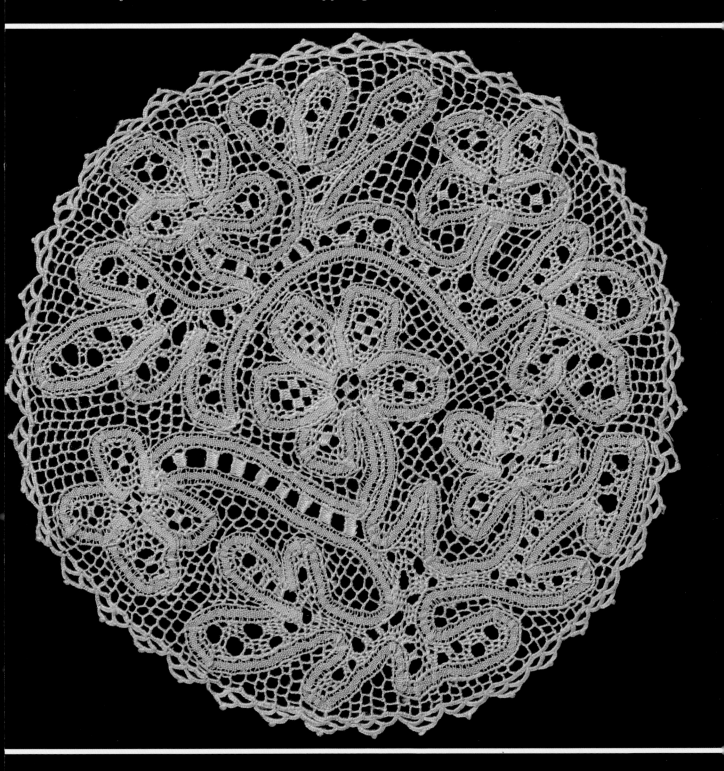

# ✳ round floral d'oyley

## REQUIREMENTS

- ✳ calico or strong cotton fabric 25 cm (10 in) square
- ✳ pattern traced onto blue tissue paper
- ✳ clear Contact adhesive (slightly larger than the pattern)
- ✳ needles: sharps no. 10 for tacking and ballpoint no. 26 for working the lace
- ✳ thread: Madeira Cotona no. 30, DMC no. 30 or equivalent 100% cotton thread
- ✳ small sharp embroidery scissors
- ✳ thimble if used
- ✳ 3 m (3 ¼ yds) narrow tape

**PATTERN**   enlarge pattern by 160%

*Round floral d'oyley detail*

## METHOD

Prepare an assembly 25 cm (10 in) square, and lay the tape in a continuous placement of the design.

Choose your favourite filling stitches from the Stitch Glossary or use the photographs of the finished d'oyleys as your guide. The stitches used here are woven block, four block, fine net with spaces, fine net, woven block bars, and net ground (see tips).

### EDGING

Work a row of buttonhole stitches around the couched edge. Into this row of buttonhole stitch work a triple loop with picot (diagram 21).

#### Triple loop with picot

Commence by leaving a long tail on the right hand side of first loop placement. Take thread across, back, then across again to give a three-thread foundation to the first loop. After covering the loop with 10 buttonhole stitches, the tail can be cut off close.

Complete loop 1 (14–16 buttonhole stitches). All loop stitches and picoted bars can be commenced in this way.

Take thread across again to commence loop 2. Return to base of loop. Over these 2 threads work 7 buttonhole stitches to centre. Stitch into bar between the 7th and 8th buttonhole stitches of the 1st loop. Stitch back into the 7th stitch on 2nd loop return − you now have 3 threads forming the 3rd loop. Cover loop with buttonhole stitches, remembering to work a picot after the 7th stitch and before completing loop 3, and finally the remainder of loop 2.

### FINISHING

Snip the tacking stitches from the back of the assembly and gently press the lace under an ironing cloth.

**TIP** Before working the net ground you will need to create an outside edge to work into. Couch a double thread along the edge design line. Now work the net ground incorporating the couched threads. The ground can be worked in any direction, however, around the outer areas it looks more consistent if worked out in short rows from the tape to the couched line.

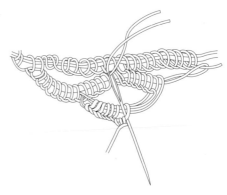

*Diagram 21: Triple loop with picot*

*Catalogue item no. 4*

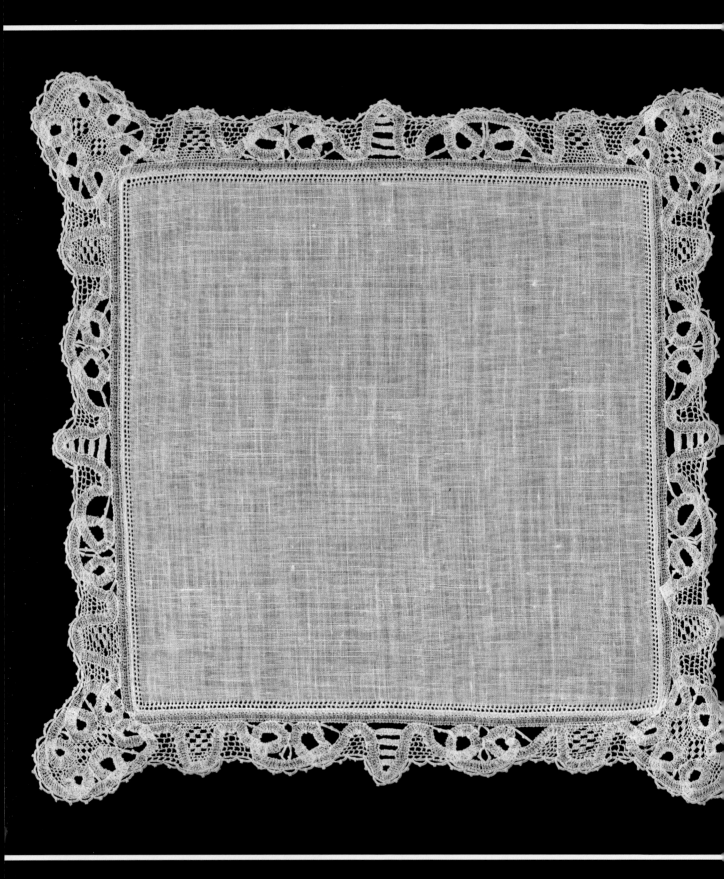

Project 8: handkerchief with fir tree edging

# handkerchief with fir tree edging

---- ❊ ----

*This lace is based on an original design in the collection labelled 'pincushion edging'.*
*Finished size: 27 cm (10 ½ in) square*

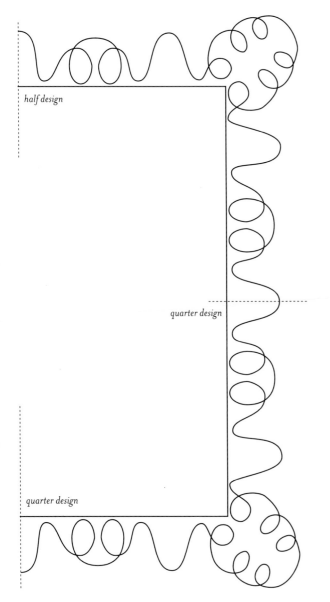

*half design*

*quarter design*

*quarter design*

## REQUIREMENTS

- ❊ calico or strong cotton fabric 37 cm (14 ½ in) square
- ❊ pattern traced onto blue tissue paper
- ❊ clear Contact adhesive (slightly larger than the pattern)
- ❊ needles: sharps no. 10 for tacking and ballpoint no. 26 for working the lace
- ❊ thread: Madeira Cotona no. 30, DMC no. 30 or equivalent 100% cotton thread
- ❊ small sharp embroidery scissors
- ❊ thimble if used
- ❊ 6 m (6 ½ yds) narrow tape
- ❊ handkerchief linen 25 cm (10 in) square

The tape we used in this project came from the store of unused tape found in the collection at Borris House. This particular tape is much more loosely woven than usual, and was used in many of the items catalogued.

**PATTERN**  enlarge pattern by 130%

# ❋ handkerchief with fir tree edging

**METHOD**

Prepare an assembly 37 cm (14 ½ in) square, and lay the tape in a continuous placement of the design.

The filling stitches used here are fine net, four block, seven block (variation of four block), woven block bars, net ground and picoted bars.

### EDGING

The outline was worked in buttonhole stitch to give a strong edge. Onto this work single loop with picot (see diagram 20).

### FINISHING

Snip the tacking stitches from the back of the assembly. Pre-shrink the linen and lace.

The linen square was finished in the same manner as the shamrock handkerchief in Project 4, and the lace attached with a close whipping stitch. Press gently under an ironing cloth.

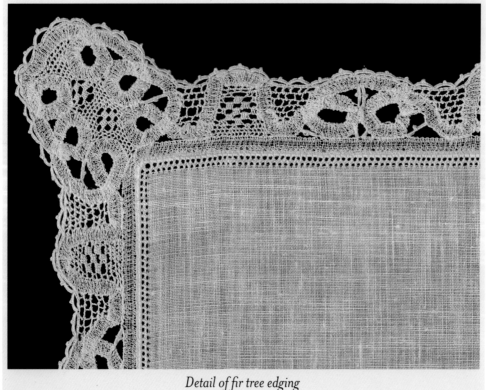

*Detail of fir tree edging*

# crag handkerchief

❊

*This design was adapted from the edging of the round d'oyley, Catalogue item no.7 in the collection.*

*Finished size: 24 cm (9 ½ in) square*

# ✳ crag handkerchief

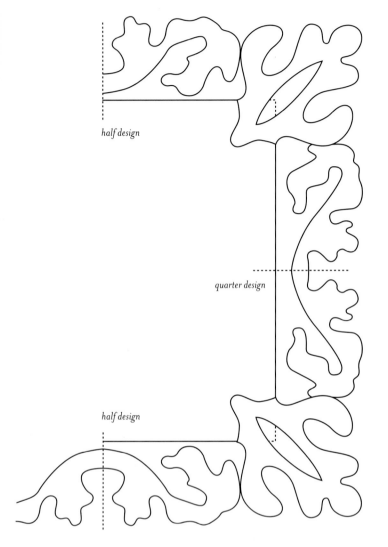

*half design*

*quarter design*

*half design*

## REQUIREMENTS

* calico or strong cotton fabric 30 cm (13 in) square
* pattern traced onto blue tissue paper
* clear Contact adhesive (slightly larger than the pattern)
* needles: sharps no. 10 for tacking and ballpoint no. 26 for working the lace
* thread: Madeira Cotona no. 30, DMC no. 30 or equivalent 100% cotton thread
* small sharp embroidery scissors
* thimble if used
* 6 m (6 ½ yds) narrow tape
* handkerchief linen 22 cm (9 in) square

The tape used for this handkerchief and the fir tree handkerchief came from the unused loosely woven tape found in the collection.

**PATTERN** enlarge pattern by 170%

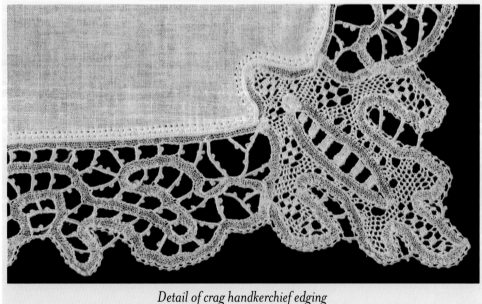

*Detail of crag handkerchief edging*

## METHOD

Prepare an assembly 30 cm (13 in) square, and lay the tape in a continuous placement of the design.

The filling stitches used here are fine net, four block, woven block bars, net ground, picoted bars (adjust the number of picots depending on the length of the bar) and woven blocks.

### EDGING

The outline of the design was worked in knotted edge stitch.

### FINISHING

Snip the tacking stitches from the back of the assembly and remove the lace. Pre-shrink the linen and lace in warm water and press both pieces.

Pin the lace to the linen and attach using a tacking stitch. Buttonhole stitch the lace to the linen with the purl edge of the buttonhole stitch towards the lace. Carefully cut away excess fabric from behind the lace, leaving about 1 cm (½ inch). Fold this back and work a row of four-sided stitch (see diagram 17) through both layers. Trim back to this row.

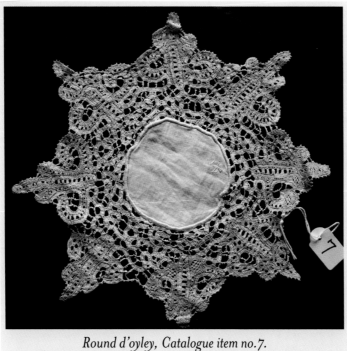

*Round d'oyley, Catalogue item no. 7.*

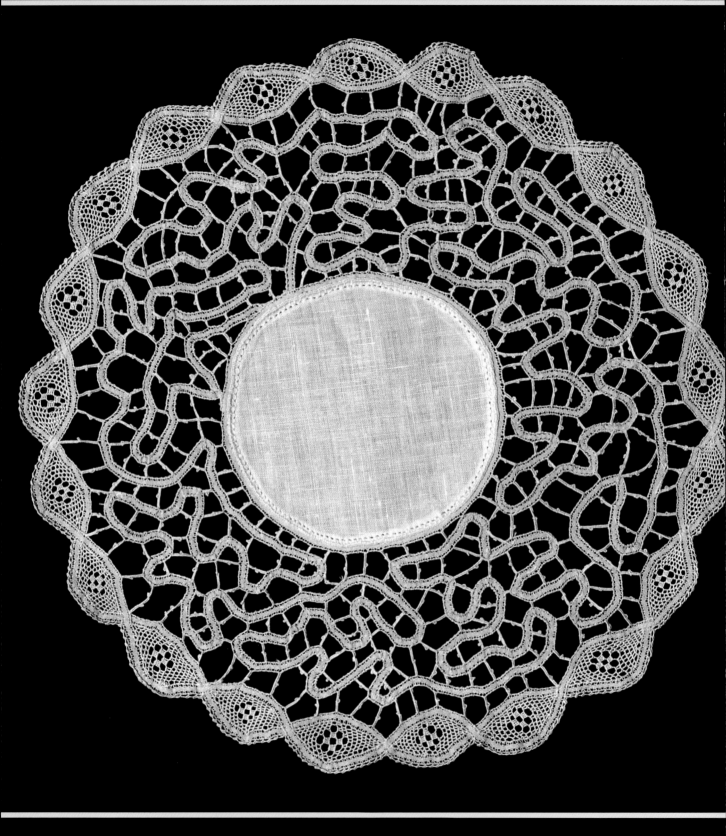

Project 10: round crag d'oyley

# PROJECT 10
# round crag d'oyley

*This pattern is adapted from a design in the collection drawn onto butter paper.*
*Finished size: 22.5 cm (9 in) diameter*

## REQUIREMENTS

- calico or strong cotton fabric 33 cm (13 in) square
- pattern traced onto blue tissue paper
- clear Contact adhesive (slightly larger than the pattern)
- needles: sharps no. 10 for tacking and ballpoint no. 26 for working the lace
- thread: Madeira Cotona no. 30, DMC no. 30 or equivalent 100% cotton thread
- small sharp embroidery scissors
- thimble if used
- 5.5 m (6 yds) narrow tape
- linen for centre, 11 cm (4 ½ in) diameter

**PATTERN**  enlarge pattern by 200%

A finished article from the same design was published in an article on Ballantrae lace in Lace (UK), No. 127, July 2007.
From this article, we discovered that a tandem lace industry was later established at Ballantrae in Scotland in 1908 by the grand-daughter of the Borris Lace founder.

# ✳ round crag d'oyley

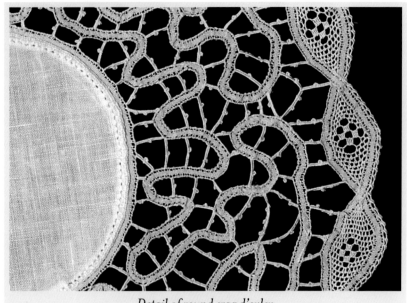

*Detail of round crag d'oyley*

## METHOD

Prepare an assembly 33 cm (13 in) square, and lay the tape in a continuous placement of the design.

The outside 'figure eight' border fillings are all worked using the same four-block and fine net techniques. Adjust the number of picots on each bar according to the length of the bar.

## EDGING

The outside edge of the tape is finished with knotted edge stitch.

## FINISHING

Snip the tacking stitches from the back of the assembly. Pre-shrink both linen and lace and gently press under an ironing cloth. Pin lace to linen and attach with buttonhole stitches with the purl edge against the lace. Trim fabric from the back, leaving 1 cm (1/2 in). Turn excess fabric back, then work a row of three-sided stitch (diagram 22) against the buttonhole stitch. Trim off excess fabric to neaten.

### Three-sided stitch

This is a neat and strong technique to attach or insert lace. It does not have to follow the warp or weft of the fabric, although the position of the triangle points must be carefully gauged when working around curves.

Bring needle out at A, down at B, repeat, out at A; then down at C, out at D, repeat twice, down at A, out at E.

Ensure that you have two horizontal threads at AB and CD.

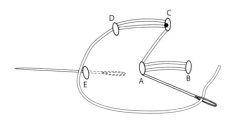

*Diagram 22: Three-sided stitch*

# PROJECT 11
## small d'oyley

*Another d'oyley with a connection to Ballantrae. Finished size: 20 cm (8 in) diameter*

## REQUIREMENTS

- ✳ calico or strong cotton fabric 33 cm (13 in) square
- ✳ pattern traced onto blue tissue paper
- ✳ clear Contact adhesive (slightly larger than the pattern)
- ✳ needles: sharps no. 10 for tacking and ballpoint no. 26 for working the lace
- ✳ thread: Madeira Cotona no. 30, DMC no. 30 or equivalent 100% cotton thread
- ✳ small sharp embroidery scissors
- ✳ thimble if used
- ✳ 5.5 m (6 yds) narrow tape
- ✳ linen for centre, 11 cm (4 ½ in) diameter

**PATTERN**  enlarge pattern by 200%

*Detail of small d'oyley*

## METHOD

Prepare an assembly 33 cm (13 in) square, and lay the tape in a continuous placement of the design.

Choose your favourite filling stitches or use the photograph as your guide. The stitches used here are double elongated net stitch (see diagram 19), fine net, net ground, woven block variations, fine net with spacings, woven block bars and picoted bars.

Ensure that all outside areas of net ground are worked parallel with the edge as there is no edge tape or couched threads to work into.

### EDGING

Notice the edge variation (see detail photo), comprising a row of buttonhole stitch covering the outside edge of the tape and last row of net ground. Work a picot at regular intervals.

### FINISHING

Snip the tacking stitches from the back of the assembly and remove the lace. Pre-shrink both lace and linen centre in warm water, and gently press pieces under an ironing cloth.

Tack the lace to the linen centre and attach, using a row of buttonhole stitch with the purl edge facing away from the lace.

Cut fabric away from the back, leaving about 1 cm turning. Fold back excess and tack down with raw edge towards the centre of the linen; press. Work a row of three-sided stitch against the edge of the buttonhole stitch. Trim linen close to the stitches and work another row of three-sided stitch to neaten.

This design was found in the collection with the note: 'Patterns and lace samples of these sent to Ballantrae from Borris on June 2'. We have only the pattern, no sample, so Marie has used her own choice of filling stitches.

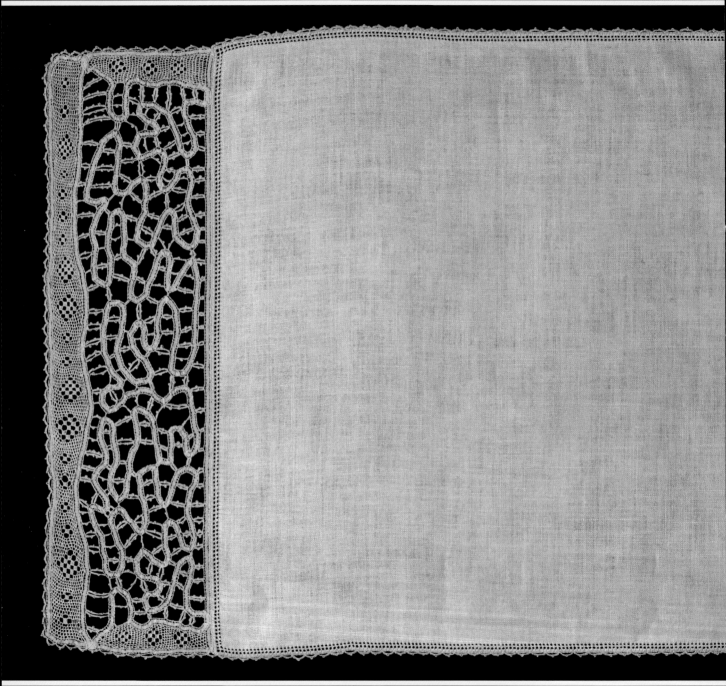

# PROJECT 12
# crag-edged hand towel

--------------------------------- ❋ ---------------------------------

*Finished size of hand towel: 32 x 47 cm (12 ½ x 18 ½ in).*
*Finished size of lace: 32 x 8.5 cm (12 ½ x 3 ½ in)*

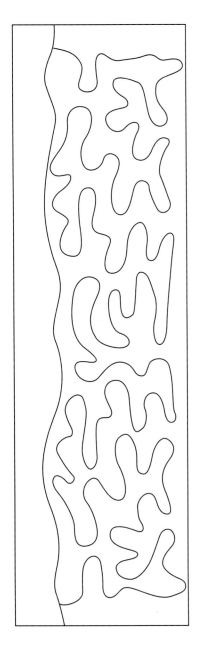

**PATTERN**  enlarge pattern by 200%

## REQUIREMENTS

* calico or strong cotton fabric 43 cm (17 in) square pattern traced onto blue tissue paper
* clear Contact adhesive (slightly larger than the pattern)
* needles: sharps no. 10 for tacking and ballpoint no. 26 for working the lace
* thread: Madeira Cotona no. 30, DMC no. 30 or equivalent 100% cotton thread
* small sharp embroidery scissors
* thimble if used
* 5 m (5 ½ yds) narrow tape
* linen 38 x 42 cm (15 x 16 ½ in)
* strong brown paper for edging technique

*Cuff in crag design, Catalogue item no. 48*

# ✳ crag-edged hand towel

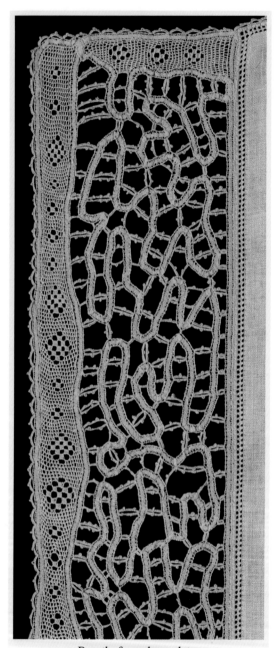

*Detail of crag lace edging*

> This project was adapted from Catalogue
> item no. 48, a set of cuffs in crag design
> with a border of fine net filling with
> variations of woven block.

## METHOD

Prepare an assembly 43 cm (17 in) square, and lay the tape
in a continuous placement of the design.

The stitches used are fine net filling, variations of one, four-
block and nine-block woven blocks, picoted bars in parallel
pairs and single loop with picot.

Refer to the photographs of the hand towel for the
arrangement of woven blocks. The ends of the design have
four-block fillings for variation. In between the woven block
variations, work fine net filling.

## FINISHING

Snip the tacking stitches from the back of the assembly
and remove the lace. Pre-shrink both linen and lace in warm
water, and gently press both pieces.

Work the linen to exactly correspond with the width of the
lace. You may need to withdraw a thread to get a straight
edge. First work a row of buttonhole stitch around all sides of
the linen with the purl edge of the buttonhole stitch towards
the edge. Work one row of four-sided stitch inside and
against the row of buttonhole stitch. Carefully cut away all
excess fabric from the outside edge of the buttonhole stitch.

Tack the end of the linen to the brown paper and likewise
the lace so that the long edges are just touching. Whip with
very fine stitches, working only into the outside edge of the
tape and the purl edge of the buttonhole stitch. While still
attached to the paper, complete the edge by working a single
loop with picot around the entire edge of the hand towel.

# shamrock placemat

───────────────────────────── ❋ ─────────────────────────────

*This design is adapted from Catalogue item no. 10. Finished size of placemat: 27.5 x 44 cm*
*(11 x 17 ½ in). Finished size of lace: 27.5 x 7.5 cm (11 x 3 in)*

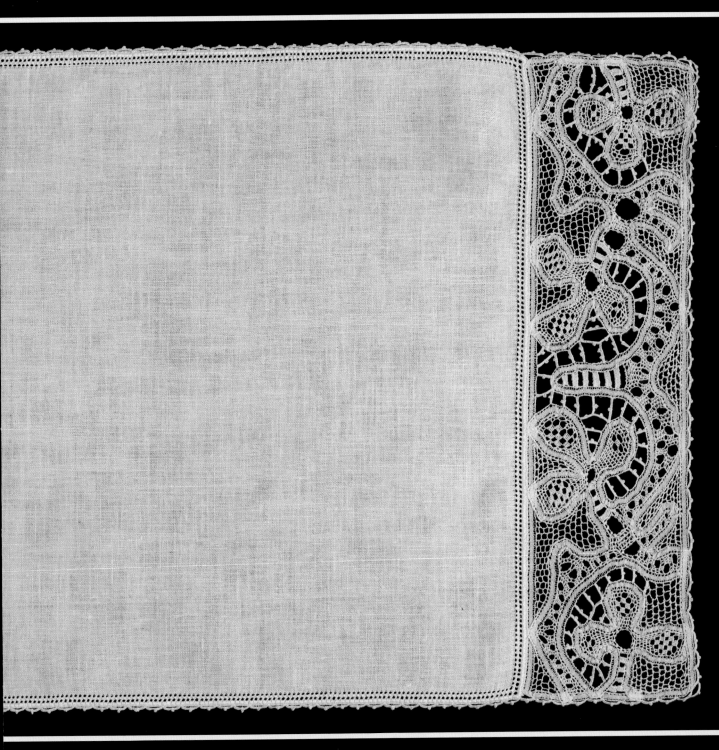

# ✷ shamrock placemat

**PATTERN** enlarge pattern by 150%

## REQUIREMENTS

- ✷ calico or strong cotton fabric 38 x 18 cm (15 x 8 in)
- ✷ pattern traced onto blue tissue paper
- ✷ clear Contact adhesive (slightly larger than the pattern)
- ✷ needles: sharps no. 10 for tacking and ballpoint no. 26 for working the lace
- ✷ thread: Madeira Cotona no. 30, DMC no. 30 or equivalent 100% cotton thread
- ✷ small sharp embroidery scissors
- ✷ thimble if used
- ✷ 4.5 m (4 ¾ yds) narrow tape
- ✷ linen 41 x 31 cm (16 x 12 in)
- ✷ strong brown paper for edging technique

A set of Borris lace placemats was given as a wedding present to an aunt of Mr Kavanagh. When the fashion of serving formal dinner on polished tables became popular again in the early 1900s, the Borris Lace Industry began to produce lace tablemats, now called placemats. A large order was commissioned in 1938 for a set of table mats for the English Royal Train.

## METHOD

Prepare an assembly 38 x 18 cm (15 x 8 in), and lay the tape in a continuous placement of the design.

The stitches used here are fine net with spaces, variations of one, four-block and nine-block woven blocks, woven block bars, picoted bars, knotted edge stitch, net ground and single loop with picot.

Refer to the detail photograph for the arrangement of the variations of woven blocks in the larger areas.

## FINISHING

Snip the tacking stitches from the back of the assembly and remove the lace. Pre-shrink both linen and lace in warm water, and gently press both pieces.

Work the linen to exactly correspond with the width of the lace. You may need to withdraw a thread to get a straight edge. First work a row of buttonhole stitch around all sides of the linen with the purl edge of the buttonhole stitch towards the edge. Work one row of four-sided stitch inside and against the row of buttonhole stitch. Carefully cut away all excess fabric from the outside edge of the buttonhole stitch.

Tack the end of the linen to the brown paper and likewise the lace so that the long edges are just touching. Whip with very fine stitches, working only into the outside edge of the tape and the purl edge of the buttonhole stitch. While still attached to the paper, complete the edge by working a single loop with picot around the entire edge of the hand towel.

*Detail of shamrock placemat*

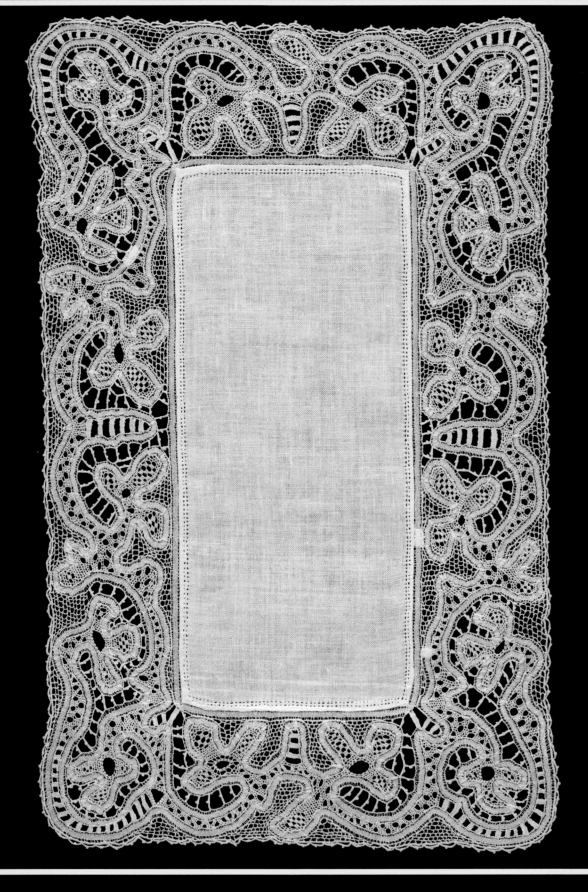

Project 14: Complex shamrock placemat

# complex shamrock placemat

❋

*This placemat is an extension of the Shamrock placemat to include a full lace edging with corner detail.*
*Finished size of placemat: 42 x 26 cm (16 ½ x 10 in)*

*half design*

*half design*

## REQUIREMENTS

- ❋ calico or strong cotton fabric 52 x 38 cm (20 ½ x 15 in)
- ❋ pattern traced onto blue tissue paper
- ❋ clear Contact adhesive slightly larger than the pattern)
- ❋ needles: sharps no. 10 for tacking and ballpoint no. 26 for working the lace
- ❋ thread: Madeira Cotona no. 30, DMC no. 30 or equivalent 100% cotton thread
- ❋ small sharp embroidery scissors
- ❋ thimble if used
- ❋ 15 m (16 ½ yds) narrow tape
- ❋ linen 32 x 16 cm (12 ½ x 6 ½ in)

**PATTERN** enlarge pattern by 220%

# ❋ complex shamrock placemat

## METHOD

Prepare an assembly 52 x 38 cm (20 ½ x 15 in) and lay the tape in a continuous placement of the design. You may need to incorporate three joins. The first run of tape will follow the inner row of shamrocks. The second run will complete the outer row of the design. The third run will frame the centre for attachment to the linen.

The stitches used here are fine net with spaces, one, four and nine woven blocks, woven block bars, knotted edge stitch, picoted bars, net ground and single loop with picot.

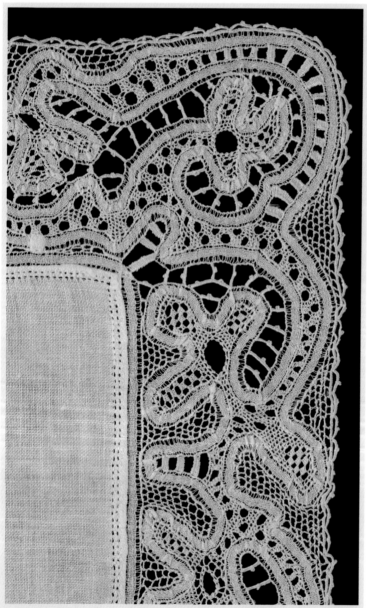

Refer to the detail photograph for the arrangement of filling stitches.

## EDGING

The outer edge of the lace was finished with a row of buttonhole stitch over the bar of the last row of net ground. Cover this buttonhole stitch with a row of single loop with picot.

## FINISHING

Snip the tacking stitches from the back of the assembly and remove the lace. Pre-shrink both linen and lace in warm water, and gently press both pieces.

Attach the lace to the linen with buttonhole stitch. To improve the look of the work, complete a row of four-sided stitch.

*Detail of lace on the complex shamrock placemat*

# fir tree collar

❋

*This collar design is an adaptation from an original pattern labelled collar no. 3,*
*dated November 1912. Finished inner neckline: 43 cm (17 in). Depth of scroll: 9 cm (3 ½ in)*

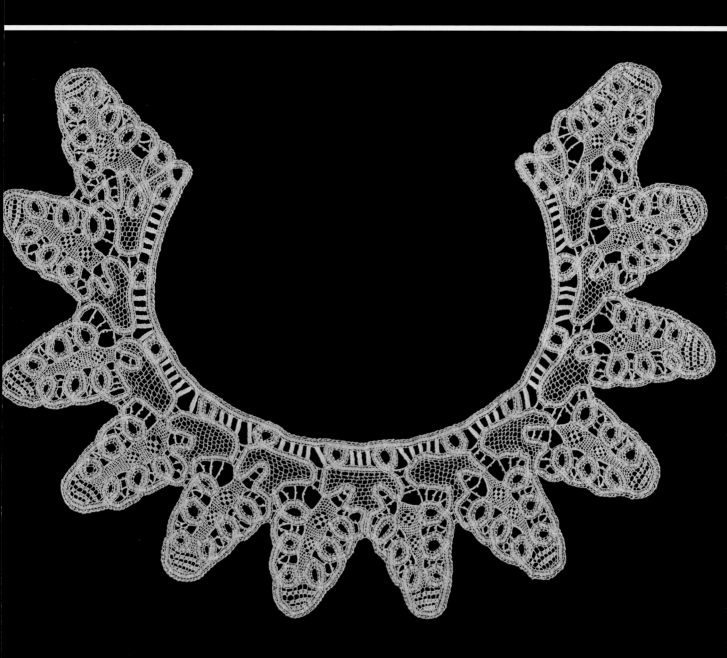

# ❋ fir tree collar

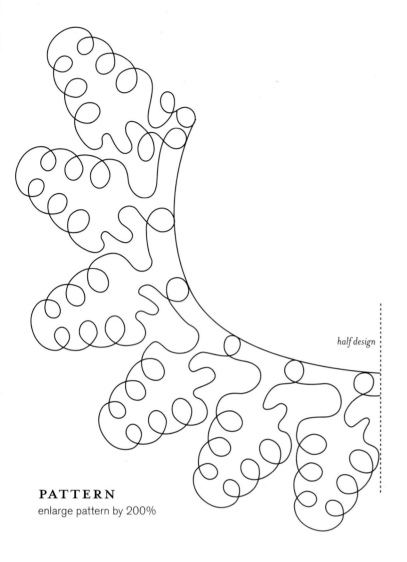

**PATTERN**
enlarge pattern by 200%

*half design*

## REQUIREMENTS

- ❋ calico or strong cotton fabric 80 x 56 cm (30 x 22 in)
- ❋ pattern traced onto blue tissue paper
- ❋ clear Contact adhesive (slightly larger than the pattern)
- ❋ needles: sharps no. 10 for tacking and ballpoint no. 26 for working the lace
- ❋ thread: Madeira Cotona no. 30, DMC no. 30 or equivalent 100% cotton thread
- ❋ small sharp embroidery scissors
- ❋ thimble if used
- ❋ 6.5 m (7 yds) narrow tape

The design can be adjusted to fit most necklines by adding an extra scroll at centre back. The collar also fits well if left open and placed along a V-neck.

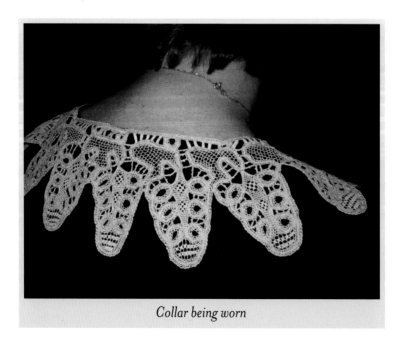

*Collar being worn*

## METHOD

Prepare an assembly 80 x 56 cm (30 x 22 in), and lay the tape in a continuous placement of the design.

The filling stitches used in this collar are fine net, four-block woven bars, net ground, picoted bars, knotted edge stitch and parallel block bars (diagram 23).

### Parallel block bars

Work rows of parallel blocks at the end of each scroll.

**Row 1:** Work a row of net ground to fill space.

**Row 2:** Take thread across to opposite side. Work 2 whips on the base thread, then work a block of 4 double-wrap stitches into each space above.

**Row 3:** Take thread across to opposite side. Whip the base thread twice then work one double-wrap stitch between each block.

Repeat rows 2 and 3 to fill the remaining space.

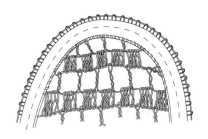

*Diagram 23: Parallel block bars*

*Detail of fir tree collar*

Project 16: Pomegranate & tree of life table centre

# pomegranate & tree of life table centre

------------------------------- ❋ -------------------------------

*This project was adapted from Stock Sample no. 50.*
*Finished size of lace: 62 x 37 cm (24 ½ x 14 ½ in)*

*quarter design*

**PATTERN** enlarge pattern by 200%

## REQUIREMENTS

❋ calico or strong cotton fabric
71 x 46 cm (28 x 18 in)

❋ pattern traced onto blue tissue paper

❋ clear Contact adhesive (slightly
larger than the pattern)

❋ needles: sharps no. 10 for tacking
and ballpoint no. 26 for working
the lace

❋ thread: Madeira Cotona no. 30,
DMC no. 30 or equivalent 100%
cotton thread

❋ small sharp embroidery scissors

❋ thimble if used

❋ 27 m (29 ½ yds) narrow tape

Stock Sample no. 50 is the
most elaborate piece of lace in
the collection and, at £1/5/6
per yard, the most expensive
border. The central focus of
the design is the tree of life,
which is commonly found in
Milanese style laces.

# ❋ pomegranate & tree of life table centre

*Stock Sample no. 50
from the collection*

## METHOD

Prepare an assembly 71 x 46 cm (28 x 18 in), and lay the tape in a continuous placement of the design. Work in sections and join tapes as necessary.

Refer to the photographs for the arrangement of filling stitches or use your own imagination and whim. This is an opportunity to use all the stitches described in this book.

*Detail of pomegranate and tree of life table centre*

# stitch glossary

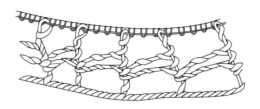

**DOUBLE ELONGATED NET STITCH**

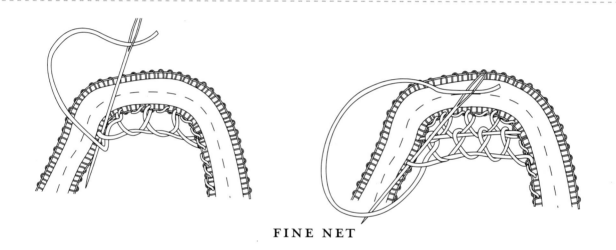

**FINE NET**

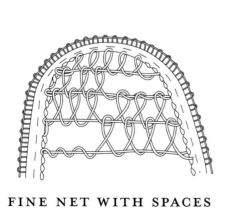

**FINE NET WITH SPACES**

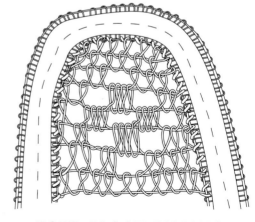

**FOUR BLOCK FILLING**

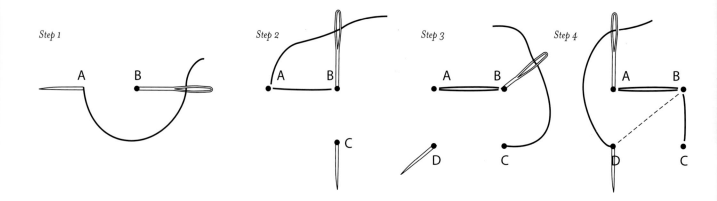

**FOUR-SIDED STITCH**

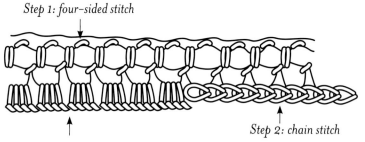

Step 1: four-sided stitch

Step 2: chain stitch

Step 3: four buttonhole stitches worked into each hole of the four-sided stitch

Step 4: knotted edge stitch (shown below) is worked into the purl edge of the buttonhole stitches

**FOUR-SIDED STITCH WITH KNOTTED EDGE STITCH**

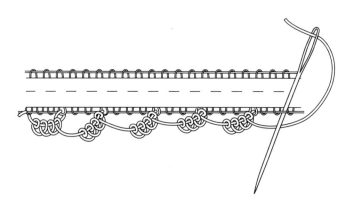

**KNOTTED EDGE STITCH**

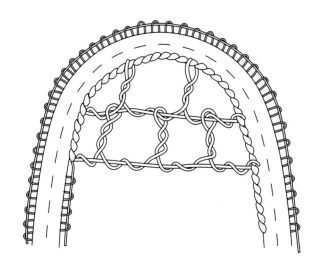

NET GROUND

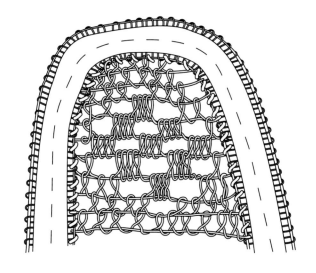

NINE BLOCK

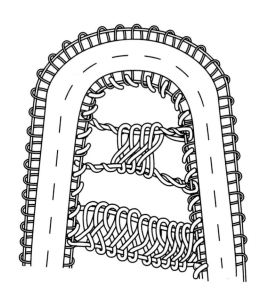

PARALLEL BLOCKS

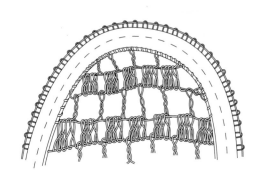

PARALLEL BLOCK BARS

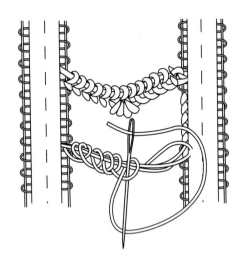

PICOTED BAR

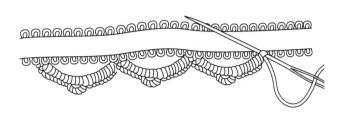

SINGLE LOOP WITH PICOT

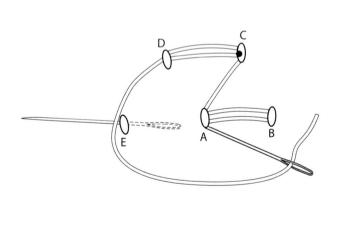

THREE SIDED STITCH

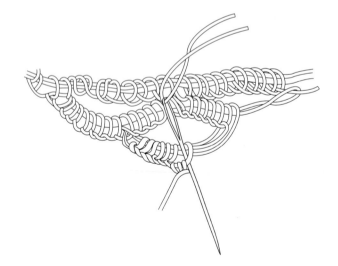

TRIPLE LOOP WITH PICOT

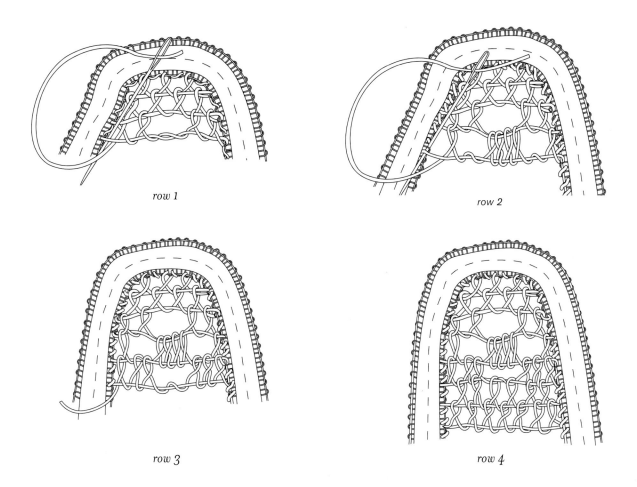

*row 1*       *row 2*

*row 3*       *row 4*

## WOVEN BLOCK

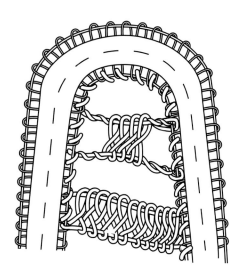

## WOVEN BLOCK BAR

# ❋ the borris lace collection catalogue

| ID | DESCRIPTION | DESIGN | EDGING | CONDITION | BARS | TAPE |
|---|---|---|---|---|---|---|
| 1 | Small square d'oyley | buttonholed centre; shamrock; spoked | tape edge | excellent | picoted | |
| 2 | Small square d'oyley | buttonholed centre; shamrock; spoked | tape edge | excellent | picoted | |
| 3 | Small circular d'oyley | spoked | single loop with picot | fair | picoted | |
| 4 | Small circular d'oyley | 4-petalled flower; 5-petalled flower; elongated fingers | single loop with picot | excellent | none | |
| 5 | Small circular d'oyley | 4-petalled flower; elongated fingers; meandering; shamrock | triple loop with picot | fair | none | parallel |
| 6 | Small circular d'oyley | 5-petalled flower; coiled tape; elongated fingers; shamrock | knotted edge stitch | fair | none | parallel |
| 7 | Small circular d'oyley | 'crag' design; fleur-de-lis | tape edge buttonholed with regular picots | fair | picoted | |
| 8 | Centrepiece | 4-petalled flower; coiled tape; fir tree | tape edge buttonholed with regular picots | fair | crossed picoted; parallel pairs; picoted | |
| 9 | Cuff | coiled tape; fir tree | knotted edge stitch | fair | crossed picoted; parallel pairs; picoted | |
| 10 | Insertion | elongated fingers; shamrock | tape edge | good | none | |
| 11 | Sample | 'crag' design | single loop with picot | good | picoted | |
| 12 | Cuff | 'crag' design | single loop with picot | excellent | picoted | |
| 13 | Edging | 'crag' design | knotted edge stitch | excellent | picoted | |
| 14 | Edging | elongated fingers; shamrock | knotted edge stitch | good | picoted | |
| 15 | Flounce | meandering design; shamrock | single loop with picot | poor | none | |

# Access Report listing of all items catalogued.

| NEEDLEPOINT FILLS | COLOUR | THREAD | SIZE IN CM | NOTES |
|---|---|---|---|---|
| fine net filling; fine net with spacings; recesses edged in knotted edge stitch; woven block bars | ecru | cotton; fine | 13 cm square | Matching pattern is marked No. 1. No edging – meant as an insertion? |
| fine net filling; woven blocks | ecru | cotton; fine | 13 x 13.5 | Matches pattern No. 1, different interpretation, same thread |
| fine net filling; fine net with spacings; net ground; recesses edged in knotted edge stitch; woven blocks | ecru | cotton; fine | 15 cm diam | |
| fine net filling; fine net with spacings; woven block bars; woven blocks | white | cotton; fine | 16 cm diam | 5 similar pieces, slight changes in interpretation of design |
| fine net filling; fine net with | white | cotton; fine | 18 cm diam | Washed, small repair – commercial lace insert to replace damaged area, buttonholed onto linen centre |
| fine net filling; woven block bars; woven blocks | white | cotton; fine | 19 cm diam | Matches pattern No. 5. Linen centre. Much finer thread: 80 or 100? |
| fine net filling; fine net with spacings; woven block bars; woven blocks | ecru | cotton; fine | 21 cm diam | Washed, set of 2: 1 x silk, 1 x fine linen centre, different fillings/makers, very fine thread/ net ground, stylised fleur-de-lis motifs form vandyked edge, fills are alternated repeats |
| fine net with spacings; large net ground; woven block bars | white | cotton; coarse | 28 cm diam | Washed, linen centre, set of 2, pattern 'No. 3 edge reversed' is a straight pattern for this item |
| large net ground; recesses edged in knotted edge stitch; woven block bars | ecru | cotton; coarse | 21 x 7 | Similar to pattern No. 8, 'No. 3 narrow' pattern is almost a match, evidence of georgette sleeve fabric attached |
| double elongated net stitch; fine net with spacings; large net ground; woven block bars; woven blocks | ecru | cotton; coarse | 22 x 6 | Filling stitch variations e.g. woven bars variation due to placement of bars. One of the new stitches is also found in No. 17 |
| none | ecru | cotton; fine | 16 x 8 | |
| none | ecru | linen | 14 cm width | Set of ladies' cuffs, linen tape and thread |
| none | ecru | cotton | 283 x 5 | Vandyked shaped edge, very fine tape, 3 yards (or 6 yds) was the usual length worked |
| large net ground | ecru | cotton; coarse | 422 x 4 | Tape is loosely woven, buttonholed edge is worked with 2 threads |
| fine net with spacings; large net ground; recesses edged in knotted edge stitch; woven block bars; woven blocks | white | cotton; coarse | 6 cm x 5 m | 26 cm repeat, some breaks, joined into a circle, top edge has been cut from a garment |

| 16 | Edging | elongated fingers; stylised | triple loop with picot | good | none | |
|----|--------|------|------|------|------|------|
| 17 | Table set | buttonholed centre; elongated fingers; shamrock | single loop with picot | excellent | none | |
| 18 | Centrepiece | coiled tape; elongated fingers; shamrock | knotted edge stitch | poor | none | |
| 19 | Insertion | elongated fingers; shamrock | tape edge | good | parallel pairs | |
| 20 | Dress front | 'crag' design | single loop with picot | excellent | picoted; twisted | |
| 21 | Stock sample | elongated fingers; shamrock | | good | parallel pairs | parallel |
| 22 | Stock sample | meandering design | single loop with picot | good | none | parallel |
| 23 | Stock sample | elongated fingers; shamrock | tape edge | good | none | |
| 24 | Stock sample | scroll; shamrock | single loop with picot | poor | none | |
| 25 | Stock sample | 8-petalled flower; elongated fingers; leaves; pomegranate | triple loop with picot | good | none | parallel |
| 26 | Stock sample | 8-petalled flower; leaves | single loop with picot | good | none | parallel |
| 27 | Stock sample | elongated fingers; flowing; leaves | knotted edge stitch | good | picoted | |
| 28 | Stock sample | 'crag' design | single loop with picot | good | picoted; twisted | |
| 29 | Stock sample | buttonholed centre; coiled tape; fish; grapes; pomegranate | single loop with picot | good | none | |
| 30 | Stock sample | 'crag' design | tape edge | good | picoted | |
| 31 | Stock sample | 4-petalled flower; buttonholed centre; elongated fingers | knotted edge stitch | good | picoted | |
| 32 | Stock sample | elongated fingers; shamrock | tape edge | good | none | parallel |

| Stitches/techniques | Colour | Thread | Dimensions | Notes |
| --- | --- | --- | --- | --- |
| fine net filling; fine net with spacings; woven block bars; woven blocks | white | cotton; fine | 9 x 492 | 4' square tablecloth edging, both edges are shaped, 33 cm repeat, loose threads and pleating of lace at edge indicative of gathered corners and removal from a cloth |
| double elongated net stitch; fine net filling; fine net with spacings; recesses edged in knotted edge stitch; woven block bars; woven blocks | ecru | cotton; fine | 25 & 30 diam | Large centre with 10 matching placemats, some have used different thread & fills; 2 pieces have high sheen thread 2-ply twist; No. 1 mat, new pattern 1924, in 2 sizes matches this set |
| fine net with spacings; large net ground; woven blocks | white | cotton; coarse | 25 diam | Yellow stain, poorly worked, linen centre |
| fine net filling; fine net with spacings; woven block bars; woven blocks | white | cotton; fine | 7.5 x 21 | Stock sampler 1; sewn on upside down |
| none | ecru | cotton; fine | 45 cm long | Stock sampler 1; some twisted bars |
| fine net filling; woven block bars | ecru | cotton; fine | 25 x 11 | Stock sampler 1 |
| fine net filling; fine net with spacings; recesses edged in knotted edge stitch; woven block bars; woven blocks | ecru | cotton; fine | 26 x 6 | Stock sampler 1; no. 29. 12/6 yd |
| fine net filling; woven blocks | white | cotton; fine | 24 x 4 | Stock sampler 1; 15 cm repeat |
| fine net filling; fine net with spacings; recesses edged in buttonhole knot stitch; woven block bars; woven blocks | white | cotton; fine | 6.5 x 21 | Stock sampler 1; 10/- yd |
| fine net filling; recesses edged in knotted edge stitch | white | cotton; fine | 20 x 13 | Stock sampler 1; labelled 'Pomegranate' 26/- yd. Two pieces joined together: top piece: dove's eye, single Brussels, pomegranate |
| fine net filling; fine net with spacings; recesses edged in knotted edge stitch; woven block bars; woven blocks | white | cotton; fine | 25 x 13 | Stock sampler 1; double flower repeat design with leaves 13 cm |
| fine net filling; woven block bars; woven blocks | ecru | cotton; fine | 23 x 5 | Stock sampler 1 |
| none | ecru | cotton; fine | 23 x 8 | Stock sampler 1; some twisted bars |
| fine net filling; fine net with spacings; recesses edged in knotted edge stitch; woven blocks | ecru | cotton; fine | 23 x 8 | Stock sampler 1; 18/- per yard fish pattern: pomegranate, fish and grapes. For church work. |
| none | ecru | cotton; fine | 26 x 8.5 | Stock sampler 1; 'crag pattern 15/- yard' |
| woven block bars; woven blocks | white | cotton; fine | 20 x 8.5 | Stock sampler 1; vandyked edge with knotted edge stitch (2 buttonholes into each loop), not well worked, mirror imaged |
| fine net filling; net ground | ecru | cotton; fine | 23 x 11 | Stock sampler 2; no. 52. Purchased picot tape edging, fine net work is very fine, tape crosses over in design which is not usual for Borris |

| 33 | Stock sample | elongated fingers; leaves; scroll; shamrock | | good | none | parallel |
|---|---|---|---|---|---|---|
| 34 | Stock sample | coiled tape; flowing; leaves; scroll; stylised | | good | none | parallel |
| 35 | Stock sample | elongated fingers; leaves; stylised | single loop with picot | good | none | parallel |
| 36 | Stock sample | elongated fingers; leaves; meandering design; shamrock; stylised | tape edge | good | none | parallel |
| 37 | Stock sample | elongated fingers; leaves; meandering design; shamrock; stylised | tape edge | good | none | parallel |
| 38 | Stock sample | elongated fingers; meandering design | tape edge | good | none | |
| 39 | Stock sample | 5-petalled flower; elongated fingers; leaves; shamrock; stylised | tape edge | good | picoted | parallel |
| 40 | Stock sample | elongated fingers; scroll; stylised | triple loop with picot | good | parallel pairs; picoted | parallel |
| 41 | Stock sample | meandering design | | good | picoted | parallel |
| 42 | Stock sample | coiled tape; meandering design | knotted edge stitch | good | none | |
| 43 | Stock sample | 8-petalled flower; elongated fingers; leaves; stylised | | good | none | |
| 44 | Stock sample | elongated fingers; flowing; stylised | tape edge | good | none | |
| 45 | Stock sample | elongated fingers; leaves; meandering design; shamrock; stylised | tape edge | good | none | parallel |
| 46 | Stock sample | coiled tape; pomegranate; scroll; stylised | knotted edge stitch | good | picoted | parallel |

| | | | | |
|---|---|---|---|---|
| fine net filling | ecru | cotton; fine | 26 x 12 | Stock sampler 2; no. 43. £1/2/6 per yd, miniature fine net work as filling |
| fine net filling; recesses edged in knotted edge stitch; woven block bars; woven blocks | white | cotton; fine | 21 x 12 | Stock sampler 2; no. 26. £1/3/6 per yard |
| fine net filling; fine net with spacings; woven blocks | white | cotton; fine | 25 x 22 | Stock sampler 2; no. 34b. Two pieces stitched together (one on top) extremely fine net work |
| fine net filling; fine net with spacings; woven block bars; woven blocks | ecru | cotton; fine | 63 x 20 | Stock sampler 2; no. 27. £1/17/3, Matches Milanese family lace |
| fine net filling; fine net with spacings; recesses edged in knotted edge stitch; woven blocks | white | cotton; fine | 24 x 25 | Stock sampler 2; no. 30. Mostly coiled shamrocks – very similar to 36 |
| fine net filling; fine net with spacings; recesses edged in knotted edge stitch; woven blocks | ecru | cotton; fine | 15 x 6 | Stock sampler 2; 22/6, no. 29. See also item 22 (same design), item 38 is finer thread |
| none | ecru | coarse; linen | 30 x 21 | Stock sampler 2; linen tape, £1/12/6 per yard. Brussels stitch, also flower centres |
| woven block bars; woven blocks | ecru | cotton; coarse | 32 x 16 | Stock sampler 3; no. 3. £1/15/6, closely woven twill tape in linen? Heavy cord whipped onto tape edge. Similar to old shoelace. Linen thread. Woven blocks (4 stitches) |
| double elongated net stitch; fine net filling; fine net with spacings; spider web; woven blocks | ecru | fine; linen | 31 x 8 | Stock sampler 3; no. 5. 18/6 per yard; Youghal spider with picots on legs, Youghal design influence |
| fine net with spacings; large net ground; woven block bars | white | cotton; coarse | 20 x 7 | Stock sampler 3; no. 6. £2 per yard |
| fine net filling; fine net with spacings; recesses edged in knotted edge stitch; spider web; woven block bars; woven blocks | white | cotton; fine | 20 x 12 | Stock sampler 3; very different – new stitch |
| fine net with spacings; large net ground; recesses edged in knotted edge stitch; woven block bars; woven blocks | white | cotton; coarse | 19 x 4 | Stock sampler 3 |
| large net ground; woven blocks | white | cotton; coarse | 18 x 31 | Stock sampler 3; no.7. £2/14/6 per yard; copy or early design, very fine net work |
| woven blocks | ecru | cotton; fine | 33 x 9 | Stock sampler 3; no. 4. £1/2/6 per yard; filling stitches are not the usual, variations of woven blocks, parallel tapes are joined with a tiny twisted bar, all tape edges are a 2-buttonhole knotted edging stitch |

| 47 | Stock sample | 5-petalled flower; elongated fingers; leaves | | good | parallel pairs; picoted | parallel |
|----|-------------|---------------------------------------------|--------------------------|------|-------------------------|----------|
| 48 | Stock sample | 'crag' design | triple loop with picot | good | parallel pairs; picoted | |
| 49 | Stock sample | elongated fingers; leaves; spoked; stylised | tape edge | good | picoted | |
| 50 | Stock sample | 4-petalled flower; elongated fingers; leaves; pomegranate; scroll | tape edge | good | none | |
| 51 | Stock sample | coiled tape; meandering design; stylised | knotted edge stitch | good | none | parallel |
| 52 | Stock sample | | knotted edge stitch | good | none | |
| 53 | Stock sample | | knotted edge stitch | good | none | |
| 54 | Stock sample | 'crag' design | single loop with picot | good | picoted | |
| 55 | Stock sample | 'crag' design; fir tree | knotted edge stitch | good | picoted | |
| 56 | Stock sample | coiled tape | tape edge | good | none | |
| 57 | Stock sample | elongated fingers; flowing; leaves; shamrock | tape edge | good | none | |
| 58 | Stock sample | 'crag' design | knotted edge stitch | good | picoted | |
| 59 | Stock sample | 'crag' design | tape edge | good | parallel pairs; picoted | |
| 60 | Stock sample | 5-petalled flower; buttonholed centre; elongated fingers; flowing; leaves; meandering design | tape edge | good | none | |
| 61 | Stock sample | meandering design; stylised | tape edge | good | none | |
| 62 | Stock sample | elongated fingers | single loop with picot | good | picoted | |

| | | | | |
|---|---|---|---|---|
| none | white | coarse; linen | 13 x 33 | Stock sampler 3; no. 2. £1/7/6 per yard; mirror image, parallel picot bars are joined, fills are not the usual; woven vandyke, 3-wrap clusters |
| fine net filling; woven blocks | white | cotton; fine | 15 x 6 | Stock sampler 3; set of 2 cuffs, very fine border of fine net filling with woven blocks (1, 4 and 9 variations) |
| fine net with spacings; recesses edged in knotted edge stitch; woven block bars; woven blocks | white | cotton; fine | 33 x 19 | Stock sampler 3; no. 49. £2/14/6 per yard; corded Brussels stitch variations with woven bar fillings |
| fine net with spacings; large net ground; recesses edged in knotted edge stitch; woven block bars; woven blocks | ecru | cotton; coarse | 23 x 70 | Stock sampler 4; no. 33. £1/5/6 per yard; mirror image |
| large net ground; woven block bars; woven blocks | white | cotton; coarse | 24 x 8 | Stock sampler 4; no. 4. 6/- each; 3-buttonhole knotted edge stitch |
| woven blocks | white | cotton; coarse | 20 x 1.5 | Stock sampler 4; scalloped edge |
| fine net filling; woven blocks | white | cotton; fine | 18 x 2 | Stock sampler 4; figure of 8 design |
| none | white | cotton; fine | 23 x 4 | Stock sampler 4; no. 39a. 6/9 per yard |
| recesses edged in knotted edge stitch | white | cotton; fine | 22 x 7 | Stock sampler 4; no. 39b. 6/9 per yard |
| fine net filling; fine net with spacings; woven block bars; woven blocks | white | cotton; fine | 25 x 8 | Stock sampler 4; no. 42. 5/6 per yard; very fine tape and thread |
| fine net filling; fine net with spacings; recesses edged in knotted edge stitch; woven block bars | white | cotton; fine | 25 x 6 | Stock sampler 4; no. 42. 6/6 yard; insertion |
| none | white | cotton; fine | 25 x 6 | Stock sampler 4; no. 40. 6/9 yard; notation 'pattern of edging no. 40 Nov. 1912' dates 4th sampler as the most recent |
| none | white | cotton; fine | 26 x 7 | Stock sampler 4; no. 40. 6/3 per yard; insertion, notation 'pattern of edging no. 40 Nov. 1912'. |
| fine net filling; fine net with spacings; woven blocks | white | cotton; fine | 25 x 9 | Stock sampler 4; no. 41. 7/6 yard |
| fine net filling; recesses edged in knotted edge stitch; woven block bars; woven blocks | white | cotton; fine | 13 x13 | Stock sampler 4. Square d'oyley, without edge 2/- each, with edge 2/9 each |
| fine net filling; recesses edged in knotted edge stitch; woven blocks | white | cotton; fine | 15 diam | Stock sampler 4. Small circular d'oyley, 2/3 each without edge, with edge 3/6 each |

| 63 | Stock sample | elongated fingers | tape edge | good | picoted | |
| 64 | Blouse | elongated fingers; flowing; shamrock | single loop with picot | good | none | |
| 65 | Blouse | 'crag' design | tape edge | good | parallel pairs; picoted | |
| 66 | Small cloth | 4-petalled flower; 5-petalled flower; meandering design; scroll | single loop with picot | good | none | |
| 67 | Pillow cover | 'crag' design; fleur-de-lis; scroll | single loop with picot | good | parallel pairs; picoted | |
| 68 | Bed sheet | fleur-de-lis; meandering design; scroll; stylised | knotted edge stitch | excellent | parallel pairs; picoted | |
| 69 | Pillow cover | 5-petalled flower; leaves | triple loop with picot | fair | none | parallel |
| 70 | Large tablecloth | buttonholed centre; 'crag' design; elongated fingers; fleur-de-lis; pomegranate; shamrock; spoked | tape edge buttonholed with regular picots | good | parallel pairs; picoted; twisted | parallel |
| 71 | Bedspread | 'crag' design | | poor | picoted | parallel |
| 72 | Table cover | elongated fingers; leaves; meandering design; shamrock | triple loop with picot | good | none | |

| | | | | |
|---|---|---|---|---|
| fine net filling; fine net with spacings; recesses edged in knotted edge stitch; woven block bars; woven blocks | white | cotton; fine | 14 x 14 | Stock sampler 4. Square d'oyley, without edge 2/-, with edge 2/9 each |
| fine net filling; fine net with spacings; woven block bars; woven blocks | white | cotton; fine | small women's | No. 1 blouse pattern. White fine cotton, hand-stitched, long-sleeved, lace-edged collar, sleeves and cuff, small pearl buttons down front, jabot, tape gathered centre back, red marking: STOCK; entredeaux along yoke and sleeve top |
| none | white | cotton; fine | small womens blouse | No. 2 blouse pattern. Fine cotton fabric, small pearl buttons at front opening, lace square collar at the back, lace insertion at cuff, jabot edged in lace, entredeaux around yoke, blouse gathered centre back |
| fine net with spacings; large net ground; recesses edged in knotted edge stitch; woven block bars; woven blocks | white | cotton; coarse | 92 cm square | Tea cloth, twill tape, fitted corners and edge in Borris lace 6 cm wide on edge, corners 25 x 25 cm |
| fine net filling; woven block bars; woven blocks | white | coarse; linen | 90 x 85 | Set of 2 matching pillow covers (match sheet no. 68) with hand-made linen buttons, twill tape, gathered corners of Borris lace 11 cm wide, matching pattern/tape to sheet, stylised fleur-de-lis motifs |
| fine net with spacings; woven block bars; woven blocks | white | fine; linen | 23 x264 (lace) | Linen sheet, hemstitching and wide Borris lace edging on top edge; no. 67 is matching set of pillow covers. Laundry label attached to 4 items (2 matching sheets and set pillowcases); all linen with heavy twill tape – sturdy |
| fine net with spacings; large net ground; woven blocks | white | coarse; linen | 60 x 60 cm square | Set of 2, linen fabric, twill tape; lace-edged on all sides 7.5 cm wide, gathered on corners, closed with hand-made linen buttons and hand-stitched buttonholes. Stains |
| fine net with spacings; large net ground; recesses edged in knotted edge stitch; spider web; woven block bars; woven blocks | white | coarse; linen | 145 cm square | 12 cm lace edging, twill tape, spiders: buttonholed, centre hole 45 cm sq, same edge but not mitred to lay flat (to fit over religious statue?). Square hemstitched linen alt. with lace each 15 cm sq. Some stitches, techniques not characteristic. |
| none | ecru | coarse; linen | 262 x 254 | 4 lace panels (insertions) 9 x 160 cm backed in red cotton. Bedspread is pieced in red and cream. Leaves grouped in 5's, appliquéd and embroidered, stems embroidered in cream crewel wool, parallel rows of stem stitch |
| fine net filling; fine net with spacings; large net ground; recesses edged in knotted edge stitch; woven block bars; woven blocks | white | cotton; fine | 78 x 54 | 6.5 cm edging sewn onto green cotton fabric with edge mitred into centre. Very faded and stained, well used but sound. |

# ❋ bibliography

Ballantyne, B. *Mary Card: Australian Crochet Lace Designer*, Ballantyne, Sydney, 2002.
—— *Mademoiselle Riego and Irish Crochet Lace*, Ballantyne, Sydney, 2007.

Blackburn, H. (ed.). *Handy Book of Reference for Irish Women*, Irish Exhibition in London, 1888.

Bowe, N. G. 'Two early twentieth-century Irish Arts and Crafts workshops in context: An Tur Gloine and the Dun Emer Guild and industries', *Journal of Design History* 2, 2/3, 1989, 193–206.

Boyle, E. *The Irish Flowerers*, Ulster Folk Museum, County Down & Institute of Irish Studies, Belfast, 1971.

Brown, A. *Lace and the Emerald Isle*, Brown, Sawbridgeworth, Herts, England, 2002.

Buckley, J.J. 'Irish Lace', *Museum Bulletin: National Museum of Science and Art* III, 1, 1913, 5.

Bunbury, T. 'Gretta Carter: Last of the Borris lacemakers', *Vanishing Ireland*, Interviews, 2008, accessed 18/3/2009, http://www.turtlebunbury.com

Caulfeild, S.F.A. & Saward, B.C. *The Dictionary of Needlework*, L. Upcott Gill, London, 1885.

Cohen, D. *Kavanagh M.P.: An Inspirational Story*, Psychology News Press, London, 2005.

Cole, A.S. *A Renascence of the Irish Art of Lace-Making*, Chapman & Hall, London, 1888.
—— *Extract from a Report by Mr. Alan Cole of the Department of Science and Art, South Kensington, Upon His Visits to Irish Lace-Making and Embroidery Schools*, London, 1897.

Connolly, S. *Irish Hands*, Hearst Books, New York, 1994.

Crowfoot, E., Pritchard, F., et al. *Textiles and Clothing 1150–1450*, Museum of London, Boydell Press, London, 2008.

Dooley, T. *The Big Houses and Landed Estates of Ireland: A Research Guide*, Four Courts Press, Dublin, 2007.

Douglas, Mrs. *Mrs Douglas's Point Lace Book: Original Designs and Reproductions of the Best Old Lace*, Judd & Co., London.

Earnshaw, P. *The Identification of Lace*, Shire Publications, Aylesbury, 1980.
—— *Bobbin & Needle Laces: Identification and Care*, Batsford, London, 1983.
—— *Needle-Made Laces*, Collins, Sydney, 1988a.
—— *Youghal and Other Irish Laces*, Gorse Publications, Guildford, Surry, UK, 1988b.

Gonner, E.C.K. 'The survival of domestic industries', *The Economic Journal* 3, 9, 1893, 23–32.

Green, F. 'Borris lace', *The Guild of Needle Laces Journal*, UK, 25, January/May 1992.

Gwynne, J.L. *The Illustrated Dictionary of Lace*, Batsford, London, 1997.

Head, Mrs. *The Lace and Embroidery Collector: A Guide to Old Lace and Embroidery*, Herbert Jenkins London, 1922.

Helland, J. *British and Irish Home Arts and Industries 1880–1914: Marketing Craft, Making Fashion*, Irish Academic Press, Dublin, 2007.

Jackson, M.F.N. *Old Handmade Lace: With a Dictionary of Lace*, Dover Publications, New York, 1987.

Keegan, C. 'Borris lace: No longer a dying art', *National & Leinster Times*, 1 November 1991.

Kliot, J. *Needle Laces: Battenberg, Point and Reticella*, Lacis Publications, Berkeley, California, 1981.

Lawergren, S. *Böttensommar [Linen Embroidery]*, AB E Holmqvists Eftr, Malmo, Sweden, 1954.

Leader, J. 'Ballantrae lace', *Lace*, 127, 2007, 48–9.

Levey, S.M. *Lace: A History*, Victoria & Albert Museum in association with W.S. Maney & Son Ltd, London, 1983.

Lindsey, B. & Biddle, C.H. *Mansion House Exhibition: Irish Lace, a History of the Industry with Illustrations*, 1883.

Longfield, A. *Irish Lace*, Eason & Sons Ltd, Dublin, 1978.

Luddy, M. 'Women and philanthropy in nineteenth-century Ireland', *Voluntas* 7, 4, 1996, 350–64.

MacLeod, I.M. 'Borris lace 1875 to 1960', *Carloviana*, 1960, and republished in *The English Lace School Newsletter* 19, 1986.

Maguire, A.B. 'The Art Movement: The recent Irish textile exhibition', *Magazine of Art*, 1898, 161–63.

Meredith, M. *The Lacemakers: Sketches of Irish Character, with Some Account of the Effort to Establish Lacemaking in Ireland*, Jackson, Walford & Hodder, London, 1865.

O'Cleirigh, N. 'Borris lace: The history of a lovely Irish tape lace and the Kavanaghs who made it possible', *Lace and Crafts* 4, 1, 1991, 18–19.
——. 'Borris lace', *Irish Arts Review* 10, 1994, 140–42

Palliser, Mrs Bury. *History of Lace*, W. Clowes, London, 1865.
—— *A Descriptive Catalogue of the Lace in the South Kensington Museum*, Science and Art Department of the Committee of Council on Education, South Kensington Museum, London, 1873.

Plunkett, H. 'Some Irish industries; the Borris industry (Co Carlow)', *Irish Homestead Special*, 1897, 108–111.

Powys, M. *Lace and Lace Making*, Dover Publications, New York, 2002.

Robinson, M.F. 'Irish Lace', *The Art Journal* 50, 1887, 145–47.

Shepherd, R. *Powerhouse Museum Lace Collection: Glossary of Terms*, 2002, accessed 24/8/07, www.powerhousemuseum.com/pdf/research/glossary.pdf

Simeon, M. *The History of Lace*, Stainer & Bell, London, 1979.

Steele, S.L. *The Right Honourable Arthur MacMurrough Kavanagh: A Biography*, Macmillan & Co., London, 1891, accessed 29/6/2009, http://openlibrary.org/b/OL7172975M/Right-Honourable-Arthur-Macmurrough-Kavanagh

*The Times*. 'Irish lace-making', 23 June 1884.
—— 'The Irish lace industry', 15 August 1885.
—— 'Irish cottage industries', 25 March 1892.
—— 'The Dublin Horse Show', 24 August 1905.
—— 'St Patrick's Day: Exhibition at Devonshire House', 18 March 1909.
—— 'Court circular', 1 December 1911a.
—— 'The Royal Irish Industries Sale', 17 March 1911b.
—— 'The Irish Industries Sale, Visit of Queen Alexandra and the Empress Marie.' 11 June 1913.
—— 'Lord Kildare and Miss McMorrough Kavanagh', 19 October 1936.

Trivett, L.D. *The Technique of Branscombe Point Lace*, Batsford, London, 1991.

Turnbull, M.R. (ed.). *The Selected Works of Mlle Riego, the Eminent Writer on Crochet, Knitting, Laceworks Etc.*, Horace Cox, London, 1904–1905.

Unknown. 'Irish lace', *The Magazine of Art* 6, 1883, 438–39.

Unknown. *Life in the Countryside before the Famine*, 2009, http://www.bagenalstownparish.ie./Ballinkillen/lazarians_church.htm

Van den Kieboom, I. & Huijben, A. *The Technique of Tape Lace*, Batsford, London, 1994.

Wardle, P. *Victorian Lace*, Ruth Bean, Bedford, UK, 1982.

# ❋ suppliers

## AUSTRALIA
Joanne Scowcroft
Josco Lace Supplies
101 Ilford Avenue, Arcadia Vale, NSW 2283
Ph +61 2 49755201
joanne@joscolace.com.au
www.joscolace.com.au

Gay Beswick
c/- PO Uraidla, South Australia 5142
Ph +61 8 83901324
dollyco@cobweb.com.au

## REPUBLIC OF IRELAND
Nora Finnigan
Kenmare Lace
The Heritage Centre, The Square, Kenmare
info@kenmarelace.ie
www.kenmarelace.ie

## UNITED KINGDOM
Claires Lace
85 North Poulner Road
Ringwood, Hants BH24 3LA
www.clair.co.uk
01425 483450

Jo Firth
58 Kent Crescent
Lowtown, Pudsey,
West Yorkshire LS28 9EB
01132 574881

Mainly Lace
104 Hobleythick Lane
Westcliff on Sea, Essex SSO ORJ
01702 306381
enquiries@mainlylace.co.uk

## UNITED STATES
Lacis retail store
2982 Adeline Street
Berkeley, CA 94703
(510) 843-7290
www.lacis.com/retail.htmlwww.lacis.com

# ❋ endnotes

**Introduction**
1 Dooley 2007, p. 68.

PART 1: THE UNTOLD STORY
**Modern Irish needlelaces**
1 Robinson 1887, p. 145;
   unknown 1883, p. 438.
2 O'Cleirigh 1991, p. 18.
3 Meredith 1865, p. 9.
4 Palliser 1873, p. 61
5 Meredith 1865, p. 10.
6 Earnshaw 1983, p. 134.

**Early tape laces**
1 Head 1922, p. 33
2 Earnshaw 1980, p. 46
3 Crowfoot et al., 2008,
   p. 130.
4 Caulfeild & Saward 1885,
   p. 472
5 Earnshaw 1988b, p. 32
6 Gwynne 1997, p. 132
7 Kliot 1981, p. 1.
8 Levey 1983, p. 115
9 Earnshaw 1988a, p. 74.

**Tape lace resurgence**
1 van den Kieboon & Huijben
   1994, p. 11.
2 Ballantyne 2002, appendix
   IX.
3 Ballantyne 2007, p. 19.
4 ibid
5 Turnbull 1904–05, p. 5.
6 Ballantyne 2007, p. 25.
7 O'Cleirigh 1991, p. 19
8 Mrs Douglas (no date),
   pattern no.8.

**The origins of Borris lace**
1 Plunkett 1897, p.108.
2 Steele 1891, p. 262.

3  Jackson 1987, p. 137.
4  Earnshaw 1980, p. 28.
5  Jackson 1987, p. 204.
6  Palliser 1873, p. 8.
7  Levey 1983, p. 115.
8  Earnshaw 1983, p. 134.
9  Head 1922, p. 36; Jackson 1987, p. 48.
10  Steele 1891, p. 262.
11  Powys 2002, p. 3.
12  Unknown 1883, p. 438.
13  Earnshaw 1983, p. 134.
14  *The Times* 1909; 1905; 1911b.
15  Wardle 1982, p. 127.
16  Blackburn 1888, p. 17.

**The Borris Lace Industry**
1  Steele 1891, pp. 261, 130.
2  Meredith 1865, p. 5.
3  Steele 1891, p. 129.
4  Unknown 2009.
5  Steele 1891, p. 8.
6  ibid., p. 130.
7  Connolly 1994, pp. 120–21.
8  Cohen 2005, p. 132.
9  Steele 1891, p. 261.
10  O'Cleirigh 1994, p. 18.
11  MacLeod 1960.
12  ibid.
13  Bunbury 2008.
14  Boyle 1971, appendix A, p. 133.
15  MacLeod 1960.
16  Simeon 1979, p. 107.
17  Wardle 1982, p. 174.

**Ballantrae Lace Industry**
1  Luddy 1996, p. 360.
2  Leader 2007, p. 49.
3  ibid.
4  Earnshaw 188b, p. 32.
5  Leader 2007.

**Who were the Borris lacemakers?**
1  *The Times* 1884.
2  ibid.
3  Jackson 1987, p. 1.
4  Powys 2002, p. 1.
5  Bunbury 2008.
6  Blackburn 1888.
7  Gonner 1893, p. 29.
8  Jackson 1987, p. 1.
9  ibid., p. 55.
10  Meredith 1865, p. 18.
11  Bunbury 2008.
12  MacLeod 1960.

**The ICA revival of Irish laces**
1.  Greene, 1992.

**Why is Borris lace so little known?**
1  Palliser 1873, p. 61.
2  MacLeod 1960.
3  Boyle 1971, appendix D, pp. 140–41.
4  O'Cleirigh 1991.
5  Luddy 1996, p. 360.
6  Cole 1888.
7  *The Times* 1885.
8  Cole 1888.
9  Cole 1887, appendix III.
10  Brown 2002, p. 29.
11  Bowe 1989.
12  Helland 2007.
13  *Dublin Notes* 1891.
14  Wardle 1982, p. 181.
15  Lindsey & Biddle 1883, p. 25.
16  Unknown 1883.
17  Maguire 1898.
18  Boyle 1971, appendix A, p. 133.
19  Buckley 1913.

20  Greene 1992.
21  Bunbury 2008.
22  Longfield 1978.
23  Earnshaw 1988b.
24  Earnshaw 1988a, p. 90.

**PART II: THE BORRIS LACE COLLECTION**
**Clothing**
1  Borris Lace Industry Account Book 1912.

**The lace**
1  van den Kieboom & Huijben 1994, p. 17.
2  Shepherd 2002.
3  Palliser 1865, p. 446.
4  Earnshaw 1988b, p. 32.
5  Trivett 1991.
6  Palliser 1865, p. 443.
7  Lawergren 1954, p. 12.

**Designs and motifs**
1  MacLeod 1960.
2  Levey 1983, plates 212–14.
3  MacLeod 1960.

**Stitch techniques**
1  Steele 1891, p. 130.
2  MacLeod 1960.
3  Leader 2007.

# ❃ index

# index

## LIST OF ILLUSTRATIONS